I0605632

THE ULTIMATE PICKLE LOVER'S BOOK

FROM CONDIMENT TO COCKTAIL—A FLAVORFUL CELEBRATION OF THE MIGHTY DILL

PRINCESS GABBARA & KELLY JAGGERS

ADAMS MEDIA

NEW YORK AMSTERDAM/ANTWERP LONDON TORONTO
SYDNEY/MELBOURNE NEW DELHI

Adams Media
An Imprint of Simon & Schuster, LLC
100 Technology Center Drive
Stoughton, MA 02072

First Adams Media hardcover edition December 2025

Interior design by Kellie Emery
Interior images © Adobe Stock/ smastepanov2012

Manufactured in the United States of America

10 9 8 7 6 5 4 3 2 1

Library of Congress Control Number: 2025942637

ISBN 978-1-5072-2540-0
ISBN 978-1-5072-2541-7 (ebook)

These recipes were created for adults aged twenty-one and older and are not intended to promote the excessive consumption of alcohol. Alcohol, when consumed to excess, can directly or indirectly result in permanent injury or death. The author, Adams Media, and Simon & Schuster, LLC, do not accept liability for any injury, loss, legal consequence, or incidental or consequential damage incurred by reliance on the information provided in this book.

Always follow safety and commonsense cooking protocols while using kitchen utensils, operating ovens and stoves, and handling uncooked food. If children are assisting in the preparation of any recipe, they should always be supervised by an adult.

TABLE OF CONTENTS

INTRODUCTION

The crunch! The tang! The salt! The versatility! Pickles just may be the perfect food. Between new dill-flavored snacks hitting store shelves all the time, billions of hashtag views, and more pickle-themed festivals popping up around the world, there's no escaping these popular little preserves.

If loving pickles counts as a personality trait in your book, then welcome to *The Ultimate Pickle Lover's Book*. Here you're encouraged to lean into your obsession—and learn even more about this ultimate refresher. In Part 1, you'll explore nearly every aspect of pickles: the science behind them, pickle varieties and their flavor profiles, pickles' place in pop culture, the rundown of festivals and restaurants showcasing the very best of this beloved treat, and more. Then, in Part 2, you'll discover the rich history of pickling and the many delicious pickling traditions around the globe. Plus, you'll find details on all the herbs you could plant to create a pickling garden that would make the brine gods proud. As you twist open yet another salty jar, you'll find out about how some of your favorite pickle brands got their start.

You'll also come across fun factoids and clever jokes that you can use to impress fellow pickle lovers, including:

- How many of these vinegary delights get eaten in the US every year
- What you would call a genius pickle
- Where the word "pickle" actually comes from
- What a baby gherkin's favorite TV channel would be
- And more!

Also sprinkled scrumptiously throughout this book are over fifty pickle-themed culinary creations for any time of the day. Eat and sip your way through Air-Fried Dill Pickle Mozzarella Sticks, Asian-Style Pickled Cucumber Salad, Pickleback Wings, Pickle de Gallo, Creamy Pickle Vinaigrette, a Dirty Pickletini, Pickle Cupcakes, and so much more.

With fun trivia questions and factoids to share with friends, easy-to-follow recipes, and home pickling how-tos, the pages ahead honor pickles in all their delicious glory. Whether you're known for devouring an entire jar in one sitting, chugging the juice when no one's watching, or constantly asking, "Are you going to eat your pickle?" this book is for you. Ready, set, brine!

PICKLES ARE A BIG DILL!

Pickles are a big dill—but, of course, you already knew that. The following chapters are a celebration of pickles on the plate, in pop culture, and more. From common myths to pickle attractions to various pickle shapes, you'll get lost in the briny ins and outs of fan-favorite pickles in this part. Amuse yourself with listicles highlighting pickle-themed restaurants, sold-out festivals, and celebrities who love pickles just as much as you do. And make sure to sink your teeth into the tasty recipes ahead—each of which features pickles in a major way. Let's dive into a utopia of pickles!

CHAPTER 1

PICKLE FAVORITES

Are you team dill or bread and butter? Maybe half sours are your thing? Sweet gherkins for the win? Whatever pickles your fancy, you'll get the scoop on every type and what makes each one different from the rest in the pages ahead. Oh, and how many times have you heard that pickle juice cures hangovers? Get ready to channel your inner detective by separating fact from fiction. And while you're busy sleuthing, save room for some classic recipes, including Air-Fried Pickles and Dill Pickle Chicken Soup. This chapter also shows love to the popular brand Vlasic, which started as a creamery business before evolving into a thriving pickle brand during World War II. So grab a fork (or spear) and dig into the mouthwatering world of pickles, one bite at a time!

The Great Pickle Debate

Pickles come in all different shapes, sizes, and flavors. Read on to see if you can spot your favorite. You may even start a friendly debate or two over which one is truly the *best*.

- **Dill.** The pop star of pickles, dill arguably has the biggest fan base in all of pickleland. Dills work well for frying, and they're hands down the most varied when it comes to shapes—spears, chips, slices, wholes—you name it! One thing's for sure: You'll never struggle finding them at grocery stores.
- **Bread and Butter.** These babies usually come in crinkle-cut chips, and they have nothing to do with bread *or* butter—despite what their name suggests. So where did the name come from? It's believed that folks used to barter pickles for bread and butter during the Great Depression. Taste-wise, bread and butter pickles give off a sweet-tart flavor due to a brine consisting of vinegar, sugar, and various spices, such as mustard seeds.
- **Sour.** Fully fermented pickles soak in a brine that has zero vinegar. The sourness develops over time as the natural sugars present in cucumbers get converted into lactic acid. This process results in a cloudy brine and more tang in every crunch. Plus, fermented pickles make your gut happy, because they contain probiotics.
- **Half Sour.** Fermented? Yes, but for only half as much time as sour pickles, so they taste only half as sour.

- **Sweet.** Noticeably sweeter than bread and butter pickles, sweet pickle brine doesn't contain any savory spices (no coriander, mustard seeds, or celery seeds). Instead, it includes cinnamon, cloves, and bay leaves. Sweet pickles are fantastic for relishes and chutneys.
- **Hot.** Along with red pepper flakes, jalapeños, habaneros, or other hot peppers bring the heat in hot pickles.
- **Kosher Dill.** While "kosher" typically refers to foods permitted within Jewish dietary laws, in this case the term refers to any pickle reminiscent of the ones served at Jewish delis around New York City. The main difference between regular and kosher dill pickles? Kosher dills are heavy on the garlic.
- **Candied.** Essentially, dill pickles are soaked in a sugary sweet, syrup-like brine, producing a treat that can be thought of as a cross between dill pickles and bread and butter pickles.
- **Chamoy.** What do you get when you blend dried fruits like apricots, mangoes, or prunes; lime juice; dried hibiscus flowers; and chili powder? Chamoy, a popular Mexican condiment that's hard to resist. And when you let classic dill pickles soak in chamoy, you've got one of the most unique-tasting pickles. Chamoy pickles stand out from the pickle crowd due to their red color and complex flavor profile.

Better-Than-Fast-Food Burger

Serves 1

Hold the pickle? Not with this mouthwatering, hefty burger.

- ½ pound 85% lean ground beef
- 1 large hamburger roll
- ½ teaspoon salt
- ½ teaspoon ground black pepper
- 3 teaspoons mayonnaise
- 1 large leaf iceberg lettuce
- 2 slices from a large tomato
- 3 dill pickle slices
- 4 red onion rings
- 2 teaspoons ketchup
- 1 teaspoon yellow mustard
- 1 (1-ounce) slice American cheese

1. Preheat barbecue or indoor grill to medium heat.
2. Shape ground beef into a patty slightly larger than the roll. Season each side of patty with salt and pepper. Grill burger until cooked through, about 4 minutes per side.
3. Slice roll in half, and toast both halves cut-side down in a large hot skillet over medium heat. Transfer to a work surface, and spread mayonnaise on each toasted surface. Arrange lettuce, tomato, pickle slices, and onion on bottom half. Spread ketchup and mustard on top half.
4. Place cooked burger on roll, and top with cheese. Enjoy!

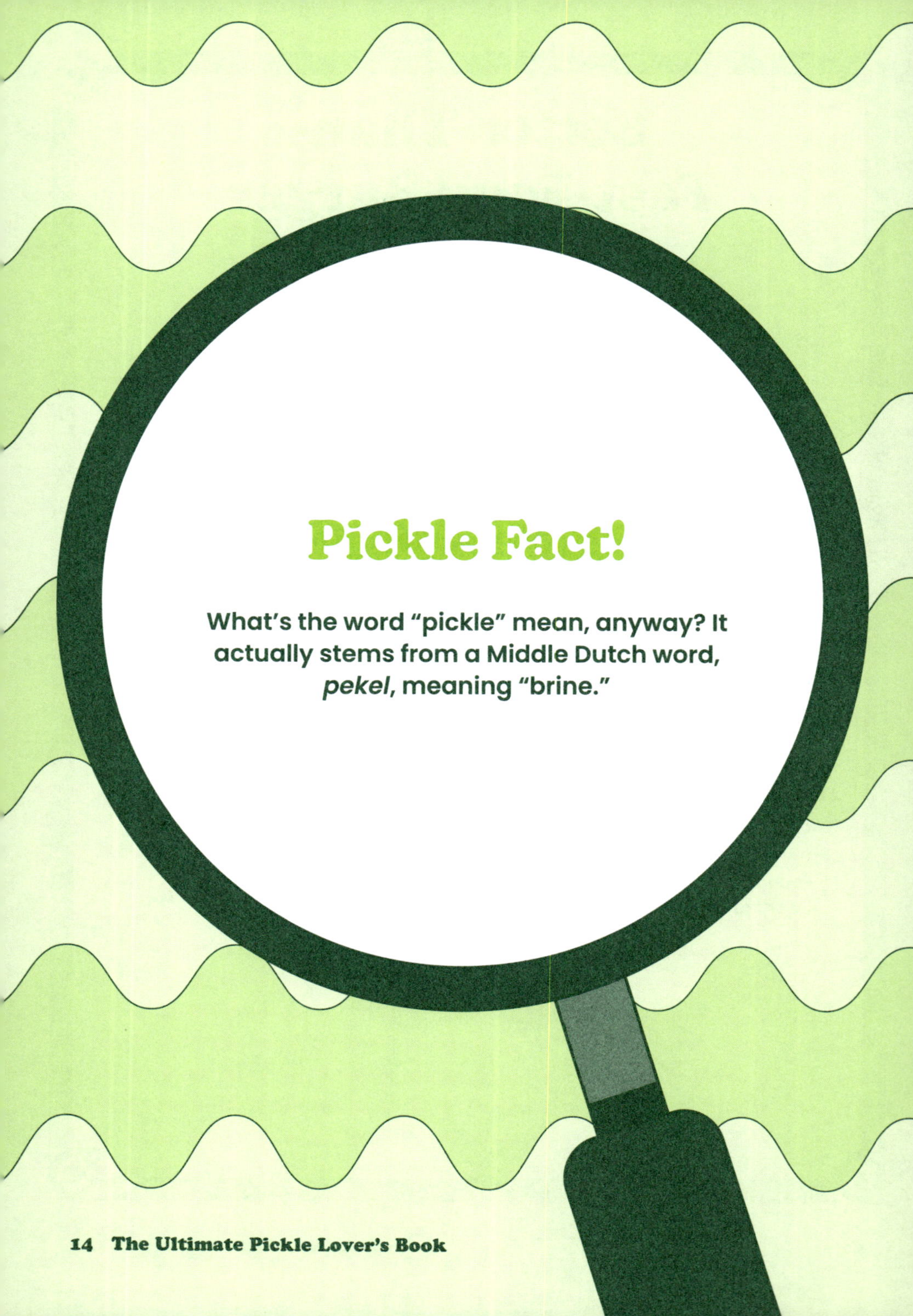

Pickle Fact!

What's the word "pickle" mean, anyway? It actually stems from a Middle Dutch word, *pekel*, meaning "brine."

Air-Fried Pickles

Serves 6

This favorite bar snack is transformed when you replace deep-fried heavy batter with a panko coating crisped up in the air fryer. Try making these with spear- or chip-cut pickles if that's your thing, and serve them up with ranch dressing for dipping.

12 sandwich-style pickle slices
2 large egg whites
1 teaspoon pickle brine
$^1/_2$ tablespoon Dijon mustard
1 cup panko
$^1/_2$ cup finely grated Parmesan cheese
$^1/_2$ teaspoon dried dill
1 teaspoon salt

1. On a plate with a paper towel, blot pickle slices until dry.
2. In a small bowl, whisk together egg whites, pickle brine, and mustard until frothy.
3. In another small bowl, toss together panko, Parmesan, and dill.
4. Using your hands, dip each pickle slice in egg mixture before coating in panko mixture. Place in air fryer basket. Spray with cooking spray. Sprinkle with salt.
5. Air fry at 400°F. Flip after about 5 minutes, then continue air frying until golden and crispy, about 10 minutes total.
6. Remove from air fryer and serve immediately.

BRAND SPOTLIGHT

It's almost impossible to imagine a time when Vlasic was associated with anything other than pickles—but the company actually started in the creamery business. After Frank Vlasic immigrated to the US in 1912, he opened the business with the money he earned from a car foundry job in Detroit. Frank eventually passed the creamery on to his son, Joe, who came up with the idea to start selling Polish-style pickles in glass jars during World War II. That's when the family business really took off!

And by introducing a Groucho Marx–sounding stork as its mascot in the mid-1970s, Vlasic not only became one of the leading brands but also drove home the popular belief that pregnant women crave pickles. Iconic.

As Vlasic's "best tasting pickle I ever heard" slogan suggests, it's all about a mean crunch. Why are Vlasic pickles extra crisp? High-quality cucumbers are a must, but calcium chloride can help preserve their firm texture. When salt is added, you have the perfect bite! Plus, Vlasic is one of the most affordable store-bought pickle brands, and just about every grocery store has them.

Vlasic was even named the official pickle of the Association of Pickleball Professionals in February 2023. Pickle Balls—the brand's snack salute to the pickleball craze—are hard to come by, but they're described by fans as "dangerously good" and tasting like "straight pickle juice" but in "the best way possible."

Sweet, tangy, or spicy; whole, halved, or stacked; big or small—Vlasic pickles are as classic as they come.

Cheeseburger Salad

Serves 2

All the characteristic flavors of a cheeseburger come together in this salad, including the most important part: pickles.

- **½ pound 85% lean ground beef**
- **¼ teaspoon salt**
- **⅛ teaspoon ground black pepper**
- **3 tablespoons ketchup**
- **1 teaspoon yellow mustard**
- **½ teaspoon spicy brown mustard**
- **4 cups chopped romaine lettuce**
- **2 tablespoons minced red onion**
- **1 medium tomato, diced**
- **2 dill pickle spears, cubed**
- **½ cup shredded Cheddar cheese**
- **4 tablespoons mayonnaise**
- **2 teaspoons pickle brine**

1. In a medium skillet over medium heat, cook ground beef for 5–7 minutes, breaking it up with a wooden spoon, until browned. Add salt, pepper, ketchup, yellow mustard, and brown mustard. Stir until combined. Remove from heat and set aside.
2. Add romaine lettuce to a large mixing bowl. Top with onion, tomato, pickles, cheese, and beef.
3. In a separate, small bowl, combine mayonnaise with pickle brine and stir until smooth. Drizzle over salad and toss to coat. Serve immediately.

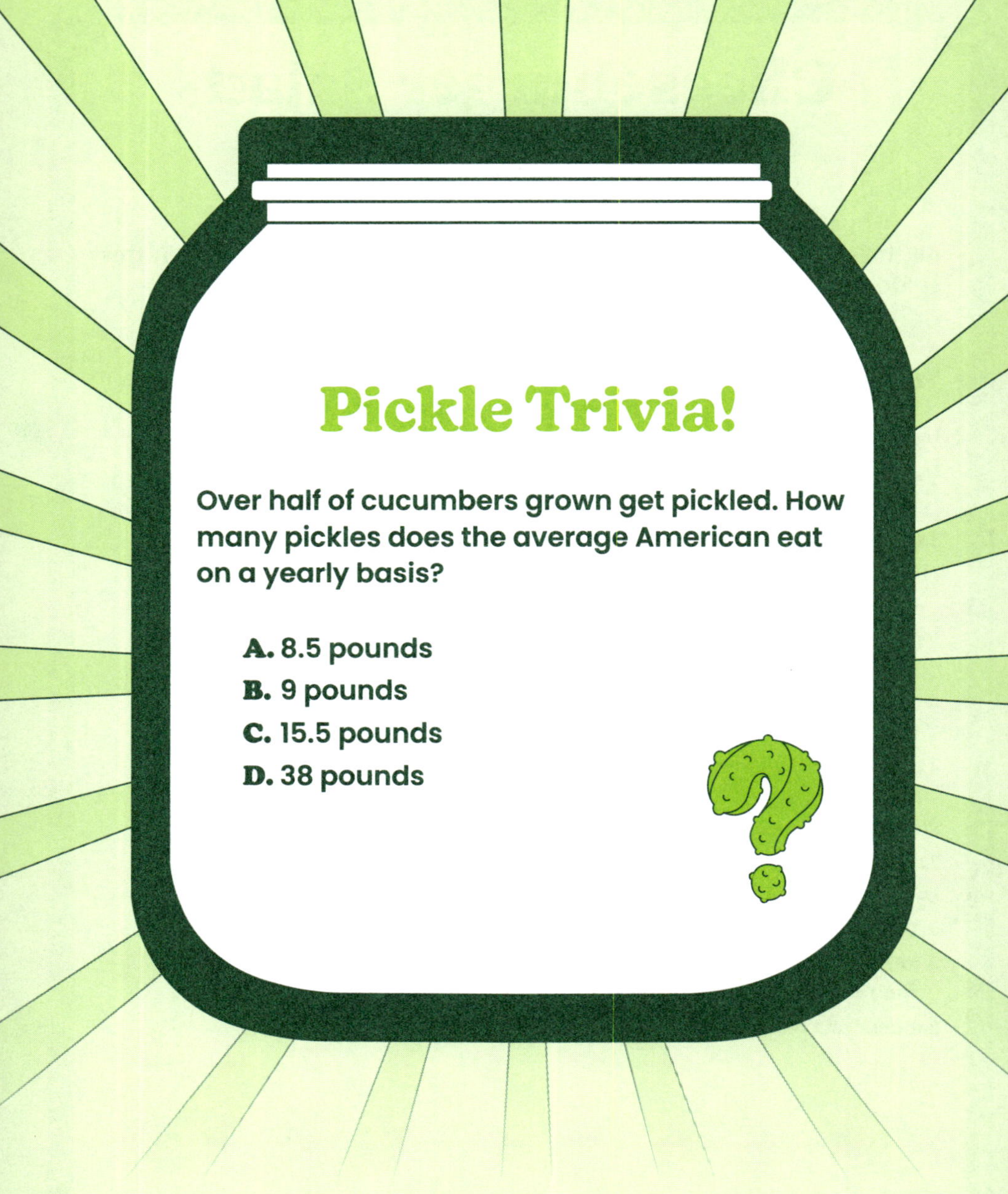

Pickle Trivia!

Over half of cucumbers grown get pickled. How many pickles does the average American eat on a yearly basis?

A. 8.5 pounds
B. 9 pounds
C. 15.5 pounds
D. 38 pounds

Answer: B. Every year, the average American enjoys 9 pounds of pickles, which is the equivalent of about 77 pickles.

Dill Pickle Chicken Soup

Serves 6

Pickle lovers, rejoice! This tart soup tastes like comfort in a bowl when you're fighting a cold, but it's so tasty that you won't mind slurping it even when it's 90°F outside. Grab some crusty bread for dipping.

2 tablespoons olive oil
1 small sweet onion, peeled and chopped
1¼ cups chopped celery
1¼ cups peeled and chopped carrots
3 cloves garlic, peeled and minced
6 cups chicken broth
1 cup dill pickle brine
2 tablespoons white vinegar
3 medium red potatoes, diced
1 bay leaf
3 cups shredded rotisserie chicken
2 whole dill pickles, finely chopped (about ½ cup)
1 tablespoon chopped fresh dill

1. Heat oil in a large stockpot over medium heat. Add onion, celery, carrots, and garlic. Sauté until vegetables are tender and onions are translucent, about 4 minutes.
2. Add broth, pickle brine, vinegar, potatoes, and bay leaf to pot. Bring to a boil over high heat, then reduce heat to low. Simmer, stirring occasionally, until potatoes are tender, about 12 minutes.
3. Stir in chicken, pickles, and dill. Cook until chicken is warmed through, about 5 minutes.
4. Remove bay leaf. Spoon soup into 6 serving bowls and enjoy!

Pickle Fact!

A cucumber is the seed-containing part of a flowering plant, so a pickle is technically a fruit.

Potato Salad with Egg and Gherkin

Serves 6

This isn't a regular potato salad; it's a *cool* potato salad with chopped sweet gherkins. Sprinkling vinegar on the potatoes while they're still hot makes the flavor superb.

- **1½ pounds yellow potatoes, peeled and cut into small cubes**
- **1 tablespoon salt**
- **¼ cup apple cider vinegar**
- **1 cup mayonnaise**
- **1 teaspoon yellow mustard**
- **10 sweet gherkins, chopped**
- **4 hard-boiled eggs, peeled and chopped**
- **½ cup chopped red onion**
- **¼ teaspoon paprika**

1. Place potatoes and salt in a large saucepan, and add cold water to cover. Boil potatoes until tender, about 20 minutes. While the potatoes are cooking, place a large bowl in the refrigerator to chill.
2. Drain potatoes, place in chilled bowl, and sprinkle with cider vinegar while still hot.
3. In a separate, medium bowl, make the dressing: Mix mayonnaise, mustard, gherkins, eggs, and onion together until very well combined. Add mayonnaise mixture to potatoes, and mix to coat.
4. Top with paprika and serve.

HA HA

Pickle Joke!

What did one cucumber seed say to the other?

We're in a bit of a pickle.

HA HA

HA

Quick and Easy Tartar Sauce

Makes ½ cup

Capers and pickles are a match made in brine heaven. Serve this sauce with any baked or fried seafood, or try it with a seafood fondue.

- 2 teaspoons (about 16) capers, rinsed and finely chopped
- ½ cup mayonnaise
- 2 teaspoons finely chopped white onion
- 2 tablespoons chopped fresh parsley, plus 1 parsley sprig for garnish
- 2 tablespoons chopped pickle
- 2 teaspoons fresh-squeezed lemon juice
- ¼ teaspoon grated fresh lemon zest

1. Add capers, mayonnaise, onion, chopped parsley, pickle, and lemon juice to a food processor, and blend well. For best results, refrigerate for at least 1 hour before serving to allow flavors to blend.
2. Serve garnished with parsley sprig and lemon zest.

In 2022, a Guinness world record was set for the longest cucumber ever grown. Can you guess its length?

- **A.** 3 feet, 8.64 inches
- **B.** 5 feet
- **C.** 7.5 feet
- **D.** 13 feet, 7.32 inches

Answer: A. UK gardener Sebastian Suski holds bragging rights for growing the longest cucumber ever. It weighed 17 pounds!

Cubanos

Serves 4

There's no sandwich more classic than the Cubano, and what would this meaty, flavorful meal even *be* without the pickle's acidity to balance the richness of the pork and ham?

3 tablespoons mayonnaise
1/4 cup yellow mustard
1 French baguette, cut into 4 even lengths
2 cups cubed pork roast
4 (1-ounce) slices ham
4 (1-ounce) slices Swiss cheese
16 pickle slices
2 tablespoons unsalted butter, softened

1. In a small bowl, combine mayonnaise and mustard. Cut bread pieces in half lengthwise, and spread cut sides with mayonnaise mixture.
2. Preheat dual-contact grill, panini maker, or griddle. Layer pork, ham, and cheese on bottom half of each bread piece. Top each with pickles and top half of bread.
3. Spread butter on outsides of sandwiches, and grill, pressing down or using dual-contact grill or panini maker, until bread is crisp and golden brown and filling is hot, 2–4 minutes per side. Serve immediately.

Pickle Myths

Pickles have been around for thousands of years, so it's only natural for myths to emerge and swirl around them. Now, let's separate fact from fiction:

- In 1948, two Connecticut men, Sidney Sparer and Moses Dexler, were caught selling pickles "unfit for human consumption." Speaking to the press about the pickles, Connecticut Food and Drug Commissioner Frederick Holcomb said you should be able to "drop it on one foot and it should bounce." The pickle did not bounce, so the men were arrested and fined $500. Technically, though, there's no law in Connecticut requiring pickles to bounce. Phew!
- It's a common misconception that, due to their acidity level, pickles never expire, even after they're opened. It's true that, left unopened, a jar of pickles can last for many years, but an open jar of pickles can spoil after a few months, even in the fridge.
- Think all pickles are healthy and low in calories? Not always the case. As yummy as they are, sweet pickles and bread and butter pickles contain lots of added sugar. So, if you're looking to consume pickles solely for their health benefits, fermented pickles are the way to go.
- In Russia, people reach for a glass of pickle juice when they have a hangover. Why? Pickle juice contains electrolytes, including magnesium and potassium—important minerals the body needs to recover from dehydration. Still, studies show that pickle juice may not offer enough electrolytes to be helpful. In fact, the acetic acid content in brine can make post-alcohol digestive symptoms worse.

Pickle de Gallo

Makes 1½ cups

Cool, tangy, and refreshing, this fresh pickle salsa is perfect as a dip for chips, as a topping for burgers or hot dogs, or sprinkled over brisket or pulled pork sandwiches. This condiment improves as it sits, so be sure to let it rest at least 24 hours.

- ½ cup chopped dill pickles
- ⅓ cup chopped English cucumber
- ¼ cup chopped yellow onion
- ¼ cup chopped red bell pepper
- 1 clove garlic, peeled and minced
- ¼ cup dill pickle brine

1. Add all ingredients to an airtight container. Stir well, then refrigerate for 24 hours.
2. Serve chilled or at room temperature.

Pickle Fact!

Technically, any cucumber can be used to make pickles, but not all cucumbers are the same. Kirby cucumbers are ideal for pickling due to their thin skin and firm flesh. Boston and National varieties are excellent choices for the same reasons; English and Persian cucumbers are great for chips and spears. Muncher cucumbers and Armenian cucumbers aren't as suitable for pickling due to their extra-thick skin, and burpless cucumbers become a little too mushy once they undergo the pickling process.

CHAPTER 2

FROM THE SIDE TO THE STAR

Too often, pickles are thought of as mere sidekicks to burgers and sandwiches, but they're so much more than that! In this chapter, pickles take center stage in recipes like Asian-Style Pickled Cucumber Salad, Pickle Pizza, and Pickle Grilled Cheese. You'll also get to read up on restaurants and towns that are known for their briny presence, as well as how two bankers turned one San Francisco woman's pickling hobby into a beloved national brand named Bubbies. And if you're searching for new pickle pairings to fall in love with, look no further than the list in this chapter. Prepare yourself for a total pickle takeover as you flip through the next few pages.

Pickles Belong Everywhere

We know these fast-food chains just love to see pickleheads coming:

- Sonic offered pickle juice slushies in 2018 and then again in 2022. That flavor option had disappeared indefinitely by 2024, when one TikToker's "Pickle Dr. Pepper" Sonic order—simply Dr. Pepper topped with sliced dill pickles—went viral, forcing the chain to keep up with the demand at lightning speed. The website *The Takeout* called the combination a "cup full of disappointment," writing that the "two ingredients almost cancel each other out." That negative review didn't stop Sonic from doubling down on the dill: In summer 2025 they collaborated with Grillo's Pickles to introduce the Big Dill Meal. Just in time for July's National Pickle Month, this limited-time menu tasted like something straight out of a pickle lover's dream. It included massive burgers topped with dill pickle–seasoned crispy cucumbers, dilly ranch, and Grillo's Pickle Chips; pickle-seasoned tots or fries; and a pickle and lime slushy studded with pickle-flavored boba and topped with—what else?—a pickle slice.
- In 2024, Burger King introduced pickle fries and a Whopper topped with (among other things) pickle ranch dressing and fried pickles—the results of a contest that asked customers to design their dream Whopper. According to the website *AllRecipes*, the Whopper's fried pickles "lose their crunch, and the true flavor gets buried in the sauce, bacon, and cheese." On the other hand, the pickle fries were a hit.

- On April Fools' Day 2025, Popeyes announced a pickle menu, but thankfully for pickle lovers, it was far from a joke! The menu featured fried pickles and pickle lemonade, as well as pickle-glazed wings and a sandwich on a brioche bun. Most people praised the chicken sandwich for its tart, crunchy pickle glaze and tender, juicy inside. The pickle lemonade garnered mixed reactions; some called the drink "surprisingly refreshing," while others described it as overpowering. And even though pickle lovers were less impressed with the pickle-glazed wings and fried pickles, they thought the menu was still worthy of becoming a permanent addition at Popeyes.

Pickle Grilled Cheese

Serves 1

Most grilled cheese sandwiches are served with a slice or two of pickle on the side, but this recipe stuffs them inside the sandwich! Take the time to dry your pickle slices so the bread stays soft on the inside and crispy on the outside.

- **2 (1.5-ounce) slices sourdough bread**
- **1 tablespoon unsalted butter (at room temperature)**
- **2 (1-ounce) slices sharp Cheddar cheese**
- **1/4 cup dill pickle slices, patted dry**
- **1/2 teaspoon chopped fresh dill**
- **2 (1-ounce) slices Havarti cheese**

1. Preheat a 10" nonstick skillet over medium heat.
2. Lay bread slices on a work surface. Butter each slice, and flip one over so it is butter-side down. Top unbuttered side with Cheddar, pickle slices, dill, and Havarti. Top with second slice of bread, buttered side up.
3. Place sandwich in preheated pan, and reduce heat to medium-low. Cook until sandwich is deeply golden brown and crisp, about 3–5 minutes. Flip sandwich and cook for an additional 3–5 minutes, until golden brown on that side. In last minute of cooking, gently press sandwich with a spatula to ensure center of sandwich is warmed thoroughly.

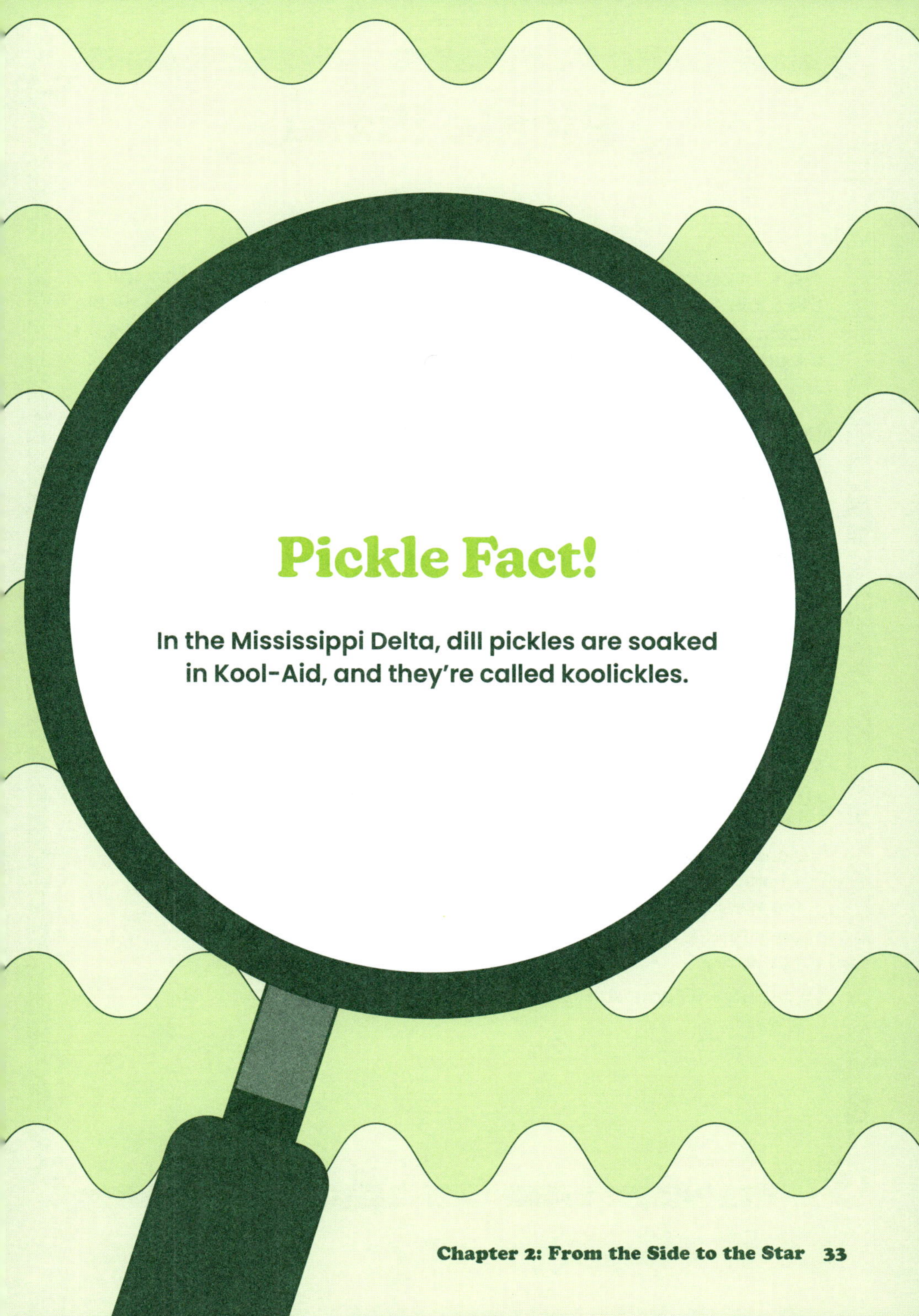

Pickle Fact!

In the Mississippi Delta, dill pickles are soaked in Kool-Aid, and they're called koolickles.

Pickle Pizza

Serves 4

Want to wow your friends and family next pizza night? This pizza will do the trick! It's covered in pickle brine–spiked ranch, plenty of dill pickle slices, and gooey cheese. If you like, you can add some sliced, cooked breaded chicken or crumbled cooked beef.

1⁄3 cup sour cream
1⁄3 cup mayonnaise
1 tablespoon dill pickle brine
1⁄2 teaspoon onion powder
1⁄2 teaspoon dried dill
1⁄4 teaspoon garlic powder
1⁄4 teaspoon ground black pepper
1⁄8 teaspoon salt
1 (12") prepared pizza crust
1 1⁄2 cups shredded whole milk mozzarella cheese, divided
1 cup dill pickle slices, patted dry
1⁄4 cup grated Parmesan cheese

1. In a medium bowl, combine sour cream, mayonnaise, pickle brine, onion powder, dill, garlic powder, pepper, and salt. Cover and chill for 2 hours.
2. Preheat oven to 450°F, and place an oven rack in center of oven.
3. On prepared pizza crust, spread ½ cup prepared sauce. Top with 1 cup mozzarella, pickle slices, remaining ½ cup mozzarella, and Parmesan.
4. Bake pizza directly on rack for 8–10 minutes, until cheese is melted and bubbling. Remove pizza from oven and cool for 3 minutes, then drizzle remaining sauce over top. Slice and serve.

BRAND SPOTLIGHT

BUBBIES

It's not a Bubbies jar without the famously cloudy brine! Known for its naturally fermented pickles, sauerkraut, and relish, Bubbies started out in 1982 as a hobby of founder Leigh Truex, a bubbie herself. (*Bubbie* is an affectionate Yiddish term for "grandmother," especially within many Jewish families.) Truex's homemade pickles were simply a hit at local stores and farmers' markets around San Francisco until married couple John and Kathy Gray purchased the company in 1989 and grew it into a national brand.

Featuring Kathy Gray's very own bubbie on every jar for that natural, old-world look, Bubbies pickles are among the healthiest on the market due to their fermentation process—which is also what gives the pickles their tangy flavor and crunchy texture, and the brine its cloudy appearance.

Even celebrities can't get enough of Bubbies! Mila Kunis praised Bubbies while divulging her pregnancy cravings on *The Ellen DeGeneres Show*. DeGeneres surprised Kunis with Bubbies sauerkraut, which Kunis ate straight from the jar while declaring, "I love Bubbies." A pregnant Katy Perry posted a photo to Instagram of herself snacking on Bubbies kosher dill pickles. Bette Midler once said she purchases Bubbies pickles by the case and gifts them. And Bubbies earned a spot on Hayden Panettiere's hot list in *People* magazine.

Of course, this brand can't be discussed without a mention of the "BubbieMobile." The "BubbieMobile" (a used 1953 Chevrolet Sedan Delivery Wagon repainted in green) was seen cruising across California for many years as it made deliveries.

Dill Pickle Pasta Salad

Serves 8

This pickle lovers' salad makes a wonderful light main dish or a satisfying side dish, and it's packed with plenty of pickle flavor! Replace up to a quarter of the diced dill pickles with bread and butter pickles for a sweet and tangy twist.

1/4 cup sour cream
1/4 cup mayonnaise
2 tablespoons dill pickle brine
1/2 teaspoon dried dill
1/4 teaspoon onion powder
1/4 teaspoon garlic powder
1/4 teaspoon ground black pepper
1/8 teaspoon salt
1 pound rotini, cooked according to package instructions
1/2 cup shredded sharp Cheddar cheese
3/4 cup chopped dill pickle
1/4 cup finely chopped red bell pepper
1/4 cup finely chopped yellow onion
2 strips thick-cut bacon, cooked crisp and chopped

1. In a large bowl, whisk together sour cream, mayonnaise, pickle brine, dill, onion powder, garlic powder, pepper, and salt.
2. Fold in pasta until well coated in dressing, then add cheese, pickles, bell pepper, and onion, and fold to evenly combine. Cover and chill for 4 hours or overnight.
3. To serve, stir salad, then transfer to a serving dish and garnish with bacon. Serve chilled or at room temperature.

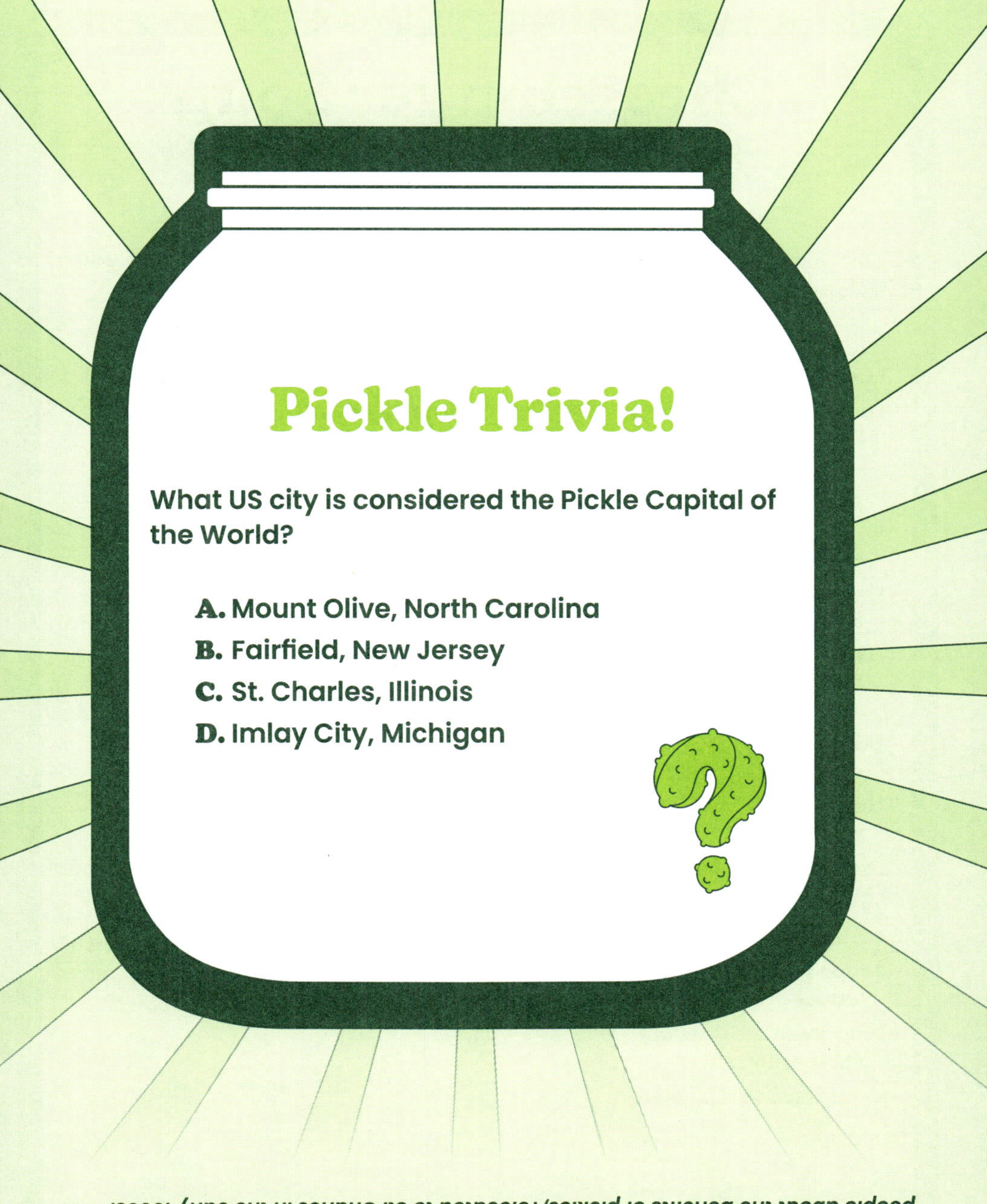

Pickle Trivia!

What US city is considered the Pickle Capital of the World?

A. Mount Olive, North Carolina
B. Fairfield, New Jersey
C. St. Charles, Illinois
D. Imlay City, Michigan

Answer: C. St. Charles, Illinois, has been the Pickle Capital of the World since 1978. It's all because Pickle Packers International, a nonprofit founded in 1892 that educated people about the benefits of pickles, relocated to St. Charles in the early 1960s.

Cheeseburger Soup

Serves 4

This soup made in the Instant Pot® hits all the same taste buds as your favorite burger. The pickle garnish is everything!

- 1 tablespoon olive oil
- 1 pound 85% lean ground beef
- 1 medium yellow onion, peeled and diced
- 1 small green bell pepper, seeded and diced
- 1 medium carrot, peeled and shredded
- 1 (15-ounce) can diced tomatoes, including juice
- 2 teaspoons yellow mustard
- 1 teaspoon smoked paprika
- 1 teaspoon garlic powder
- ½ teaspoon salt
- 4 cups beef broth
- 2 cups shredded iceberg lettuce
- 1 cup shredded Cheddar cheese, divided
- ½ cup diced dill pickles

1. Press Sauté button on Instant Pot®, and heat oil for 30 seconds. Add beef, onion, and green pepper to pot. Sauté for 5 minutes, or until beef begins to brown. Add carrot and heat for an additional minute.
2. Add tomatoes, mustard, paprika, garlic powder, salt, and beef broth to pot. Lock lid.
3. Press the Manual or Pressure Cook button, and adjust cook time to 7 minutes. When timer beeps, quick-release pressure until float valve drops, and then unlock lid.
4. Stir in lettuce and ½ cup cheese, and simmer for 3 minutes.
5. Ladle soup into bowls, and garnish with diced dill pickles and remaining ½ cup cheese. Serve warm.

HA HA
Pickle Joke!
Why did the cucumber blush?
It saw the salad dressing!
HA
HA
HA

Nashville Hot Chicken

Serves 4

Get your deep fryer ready, because this dish has it all: heat, sweetness, and tangy pickles! The chicken is brined with dill pickle juice and hot sauce, dunked in Nashville hot sauce, and garnished with pickle slices.

For Chicken

- 4 (6-ounce) boneless, skinless chicken breasts
- 1/4 cup buttermilk
- 1/4 cup dill pickle brine
- 2 tablespoons hot sauce
- 1 teaspoon granulated sugar
- Vegetable oil, for frying
- 1 1/2 cups all-purpose flour
- 2 teaspoons ground black pepper
- 1 1/2 teaspoons salt
- 1 1/2 teaspoons paprika

For Nashville Hot Sauce

- 1/4 cup cayenne pepper
- 3 tablespoons packed light brown sugar
- 1 tablespoon paprika
- 1/2 teaspoon garlic powder
- 1/2 teaspoon onion powder
- 1/2 cup hot frying oil

For Garnish

- 12 dill pickle slices

1. To make chicken, in a 1-gallon resealable plastic bag, combine chicken, buttermilk, pickle brine, hot sauce, and sugar. Seal bag, removing as much air as you can, and massage to combine marinade ingredients and evenly coat chicken. Refrigerate for at least 2 hours and up to 24 hours.
2. Remove chicken from refrigerator 30 minutes before cooking to warm to room temperature.

3. Fill deep fryer with oil per manufacturer instructions and heat to 350°F, or fill a 5½-quart Dutch oven with oil 3" deep, leaving at least 3" of space at top, and place over medium-high heat until oil reaches 350°F.
4. To a medium bowl, add flour, pepper, salt, and paprika and mix well. Remove chicken from marinade, letting excess drip off. Dredge chicken in flour mixture, shaking off excess flour. Place chicken on a rack and let stand for 5 minutes, then return to flour mixture and coat again.
5. Gently place chicken in hot oil. Fry for 5–7 minutes, until chicken reaches an internal temperature of 165°F. Do not crowd pot. Work in batches if needed. Remove chicken from oil and let drain on a paper towel–lined plate.
6. To make Nashville hot sauce, in a 1-quart saucepan over low heat, combine cayenne pepper, sugar, paprika, garlic powder, onion powder, and hot frying oil. Whisk until smooth. Cook for 3 minutes, making sure the sauce does not start to bubble. Remove from heat and cool for 2 minutes.
7. Place chicken breasts in sauce, and turn to coat evenly. Transfer chicken to a serving platter and top with pickle slices. Serve immediately.

Pickle Fact!

In some Southern states, like Texas, Louisiana, and Oklahoma, whole pickles are sold at movie theater concession stands.

Pickle Pairings

Your guests won't leave disappointed if you pair pickles with any of these delicious treats at your next hangout:

- **Grilled Cheese.** As if the texture contrast between ooey, gooey cheese and warm, crisp, buttery bread weren't satisfying enough, adding pickles to the equation takes it up several notches. Bread and butter pickles are a common first choice for this pairing; the sweetness and tanginess balance the savory cheeses. But if bread and butter pickles really aren't your thing, the tanginess of dill pickles complement the sharpness of Cheddar or goat cheese. And who says the pickles have to sit on the sidelines? Layer on a handful of sliced pickles right as the cheese is melting onto the bread to marry the flavors together.
- **Buffalo Wings.** Wings are as fun as they are yummy to eat. In the US, buffalo is the most popular wing flavor. Buffalo wings are both tangy and a little spicy, so they go well with the bright, tangy flavor of dill pickles. And while ranch and blue cheese dipping sauces are must-haves, try dunking your wings directly into the pickle juice for an extra burst of flavor.
- **Charcuterie Board.** On a charcuterie board, you'll find an assortment of finger foods: cured meats like prosciutto and salami; cheeses; olives; fruits like pears, grapes, and dried figs; nuts; pretzels; crackers; and, most importantly, pickles. Cornichons are a great choice for the tartness and crunchy texture they bring. And because cornichons are so small, they're easy to crunch on between nibbles of all the other bite-sized goodies on your charcuterie board.

- **Pizza.** Say hello to your new favorite pizza topping. The salty, tangy goodness of the pickles—dill is a fan favorite—offers a nice contrast to the sweet marinara sauce. The acidity also cuts through the richness and fat content of the meats and cheese. Like their more traditional pizza-topping cousin the banana pepper, pickles bring bright, zesty flavor to every slice.
- **Beer.** Pickles and a pint of beer just sound like they were meant to go together. The type of pickle to pair a beer with all depends on the flavor notes. Pale ales and wheat beers have citrusy, earthy undertones and a slight bitterness, making fried dill pickles the best choice. You can also combine fried pickles with stouts, known for having layers of chocolate, coffee, or caramel. IPAs are noticeably more bitter than other types of beer, so spicy pickles complement them beautifully (and vice versa). If you can handle it, you can even pair an IPA with pickled jalapeños. And if you open your fridge to find a jar of full sour or half sour pickles staring back at you, eat them while sipping on an acidic beer—for example, a sour ale such as a Gose or Berliner Weisse.

Asian-Style Pickled Cucumber Salad

Serves 8

If spicy yellow curries or rich, nutty satays are the stars of your meal, this is the side dish your taste buds need.

- **1/3 cup white vinegar**
- **1/3 cup granulated sugar**
- **1/2 cup water**
- **1 teaspoon salt**
- **3 medium thin-skinned cucumbers, quartered and thinly sliced**
- **1 medium shallot, peeled and thinly sliced**
- **1 teaspoon minced ginger**
- **1/4 cup chopped fresh cilantro**

1. In a medium saucepan, bring vinegar, sugar, water, and salt to a boil over high heat to dissolve sugar. Turn off heat and let cool.
2. In a large mixing bowl, combine cucumbers, shallot, ginger, and cilantro and toss well with dressing. Let salad rest for 20 minutes before serving.

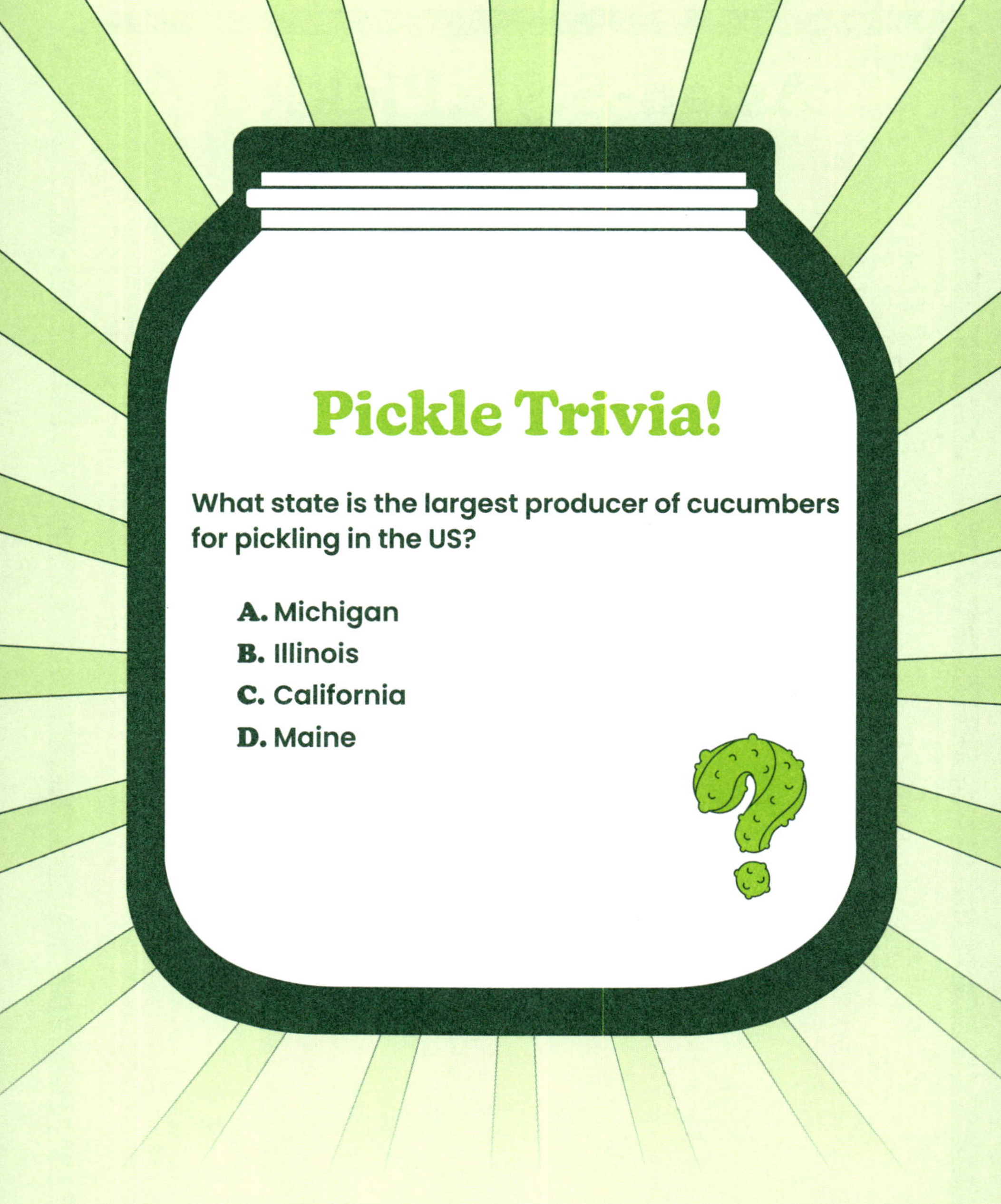

Pickle Trivia!

What state is the largest producer of cucumbers for pickling in the US?

- **A.** Michigan
- **B.** Illinois
- **C.** California
- **D.** Maine

Answer: A. Michigan grows the most pickling cucumbers, due to its sandy soils and mild temperatures. The state produces about 216,000 tons of pickling cucumbers each year.

Cubano Pork Chops

Serves 2

Made in the Instant Pot®, this one-pot dish contains every great flavor found in the classic Cuban-style sandwich. Don't skip the pickle slices—they bring the dish to life.

2 (3/4-pound, about 1"-thick) boneless pork chops
2 tablespoons yellow mustard
1 tablespoon olive oil
2 cups water
4 (0.5-ounce) slices ham
8 dill pickle slices
4 (1-ounce) slices Swiss cheese

1. Slather all sides of pork chops with mustard. Set aside.
2. Press Sauté button on Instant Pot® and add oil. Once hot, add chops and brown well on both sides, about 2–3 minutes per side. Remove from pot and place chops on a plate.
3. Pour water into pot and scrape any brown bits from bottom of pot. Once bottom of pot is free from any brown bits, press Cancel. Add steam rack to pot, and place pork chops on rack. Close lid, set steam release to Sealing, press Manual, and set time to 13 minutes.
4. Once cooking is complete, quick-release pressure. Press Cancel and open lid. Add ham slices and dill pickle slices atop pork chops. Cover with Swiss cheese. Close lid and let residual heat from cooking melt cheese, about 2–3 minutes. Serve warm.

Pickle Fact!

On Chicago's South Side, it's common to put a peppermint stick lengthwise through the middle of a pickle for a sweet, salty, and sour combo.

Pickle Landmarks Around the World

From the buildings you pass every day to the restaurants you love, pickle history is all around you!

- Built in 1888, the Pickle Works Building in Los Angeles was home to California Vinegar & Pickle Company until 1909. It was one of the oldest buildings in the downtown L.A. Arts District until its demolition after a 2018 fire.
- West Perth, Australia's Pickle District is now a bustling arts hub with galleries and design studios, but in 1917 it was home to Tandy's Preserves and Pickle Factory.
- The Eiffel Tower is breathtaking, but don't underestimate the beauty of a 14-foot-tall pickle sporting a Santa hat. The world's largest Christmas pickle lives in Arkansas, and it's become a popular roadside attraction.
- In the late nineteenth and early twentieth centuries, Essex Street in Lower Manhattan was known as Pickle Alley, because it was home to dozens of pickle vendors. And while the tangy scent of pickle brine in the streets is gone, The Pickle Guys honors that rich history one jar at a time. Located right on Essex Street, this gourmet grocery store has all the basics: sour, half sour, hot sour, bread and butter, sweet gherkins, and pickle brine by the gallon. You can also purchase pickled okra, Brussels sprouts, turnips, mushrooms, baby corn, and cherry peppers.

- At Jacob's Pickles in New York City, "A pickle is more than just a pickle." With menu items like hot sour cucumbers, dilly green beans, pickled eggs, fried pickles, pickle slaw, a spicy brine margarita, and pickle ice cream with actual pickle slices, you know it's the real dill. In fact, all the pickles are made in-house.
- Elsie's, a sub shop in New Jersey, became big on TikTok for serving sandwiches on pickles. The homemade, house-cured pickle halves are hollowed out to make room for all the fillings. Elsie's also serves up tasty pickle and cucumber roll-ups.
- You can taste the pickle rainbow at Wut-A-Pickle, a California pickle eatery where unique flavors like grape, green apple, pineapple, peach mango, spicy tropical punch, strawberry, watermelon, peppermint, and blue raspberry lemonade are just a bite away.
- The only thing better than a pickle is a pickle boat. Kaylin + Kaylin made a name for itself by opening Los Angeles's first pickle tasting bar and they've found a way to top themselves—literally. Indulge in a boat-shaped pickle half topped with a savory combo of cream cheese, lox, and capers—or a sweet layering of peanut butter, Nutella, and pretzels. Now, that's something to relish!

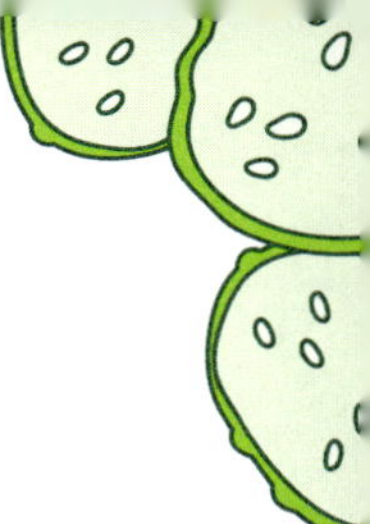

CHAPTER 3

PICKLES ARE A PARTY!

Sometimes being in a pickle is a good thing! From festivals held in the Christmas Pickle Capital of the World to a get-together where a Mayor of Picklesburgh is crowned, the pickle revolution is front and center in the following chapter. And if you're bringing the party to *your* place, you're going to need some dill-licious recipes. Whether you're throwing a pickle-themed party or not, who wouldn't appreciate a Dirty Pickletini? Add Pickleback Wings and Air-Fried Dill Pickle Mozzarella Sticks to the menu and your guests will be raving for the rest of the year. You'll also dive down the rabbit hole of fun pickle facts, find out how Mt. Olive became the biggest independent pickle maker in the US, and get a quick guide to pickle shapes.

Pickle Festivals Around the World

There's no such thing as too many pickle-themed festivals, so grab your wristbands and check out these events:

- **Berrien Springs Pickle Festival.** What does a small town do after being nicknamed the Christmas Pickle Capital of the World? Throw a pickle festival, of course! Held annually on July 4, Michigan's Berrien Springs Pickle Festival is inspired by Berrien Springs's notable history of German immigration via the quirky tradition of hanging pickle ornaments on Christmas trees. (Find out more about the Christmas pickle tradition in Chapter 4.) From pickle tossing (the current pickle fling world record distance is 292 feet) to pickle eating and decorating contests, this festival offers much to relish.
- **In a Pickle Festival.** Pickle pizza, pickle snow cones, pickle beer, pickle cotton candy, pickle cupcakes, and pickle popcorn—these are just a tiny sampling of the briny treats you'll find at the In a Pickle Festival in Kingwood, Texas. There's even a pickle canning contest and a Pickled Pet Parade, where the best-dressed pups win prizes. Created in response to Hurricane Harvey, which left many business owners in a tricky spot, the festival also raises money for the rare genetic disease Hunter Syndrome.
- **The Big Dill.** Billed as the world's largest pickle party, The Big Dill is so much more than a pickle festival. Of course, you've got your pickle fudge, pickle cookies, pickle corn dogs, pickle grilled cheese, and pickle egg rolls, as well as plenty of pickle-themed

photo opps and merch. But with half a million pickles eaten since 2019, it's a pickle movement that's taking over the globe. It started off in Baltimore and has quickly expanded to Philadelphia and Arlington, Texas. So, if pickles are in your DNA, then wear your most comfortable shoes, because there's an invite with your name on it.

- **Picklesburgh.** The minute you spot the 35-foot-long Heinz pickle balloon in the sky, you know you're in the right place. Pittsburgh has been synonymous with pickles since Henry J. Heinz was known as the Pickle King in the 1800s. Heinz was one of the first companies to bottle pickles. At Picklesburgh, come for the pickled chicken wings and Mexican street corn pickles, but stay for the chance to get crowned Mayor of Picklesburgh and walk away with $500. All you have to do is finish chugging down an entire quart-sized jar of pickle juice before everyone else.

Chicago-Style Hot Dog

Serves 1

Chicago-style dogs are a Chicago staple as well as a pickle lover's dream. Each dog is topped with sweet relish *and* a whole dill pickle spear, along with plenty of other fresh toppings. One reminder: Never add ketchup to a Chicago dog!

1 all-beef hot dog
1 hot dog bun
2 teaspoons yellow mustard
1 tablespoon sweet pickle relish
1 tablespoon finely chopped white onion
1 (1/8") slice from a large tomato, cut into half-moons
1 dill pickle spear
2 sport peppers
1/4 teaspoon celery salt

1. To a 2-quart saucepan, add hot dog and enough water to cover. Heat over high heat until water comes to a boil, then turn off heat, cover, and let stand for 5 minutes.
2. Heat hot dog bun for 8 seconds on High in microwave. Place on a plate, open bun, and spread inside with mustard. Add hot dog, then add remaining toppings. Serve immediately.

Pickle Fact!

Is that little pickle a cornichon or a gherkin—or maybe both? Here's the story: It turns out that a cornichon is actually a young gherkin cucumber. Because their distinctive flavor comes from spices and herbs, such as coriander, pepper, and tarragon, cornichons have a tartness and slight herbal taste that isn't found in gherkins, which heavily rely on dill and garlic for their sourness. Sometimes called French gherkins, cornichons are harvested before they fully develop. This means they're also smaller (about 1"–2" long) in size and bumpier in texture.

Air-Fried Dill Pickle Mozzarella Sticks

Serves 6

Craving fried pickles one minute and golden mozzarella sticks the next? Now you can have both! Use the brine from your favorite jar of dill pickles to really make this recipe pop.

1 large egg white
2 teaspoons dill pickle brine
1 cup panko
½ cup finely grated Parmesan cheese
1 teaspoon dried dill
1 teaspoon salt
6 (1-ounce) mozzarella cheese sticks

1. In a small bowl, beat together egg white and pickle brine until frothy.
2. In another small bowl, toss together panko, Parmesan, dill, and salt.
3. Using your hands, dip a cheese stick in the egg mixture and then coat in bread crumbs. Place on a plate. Repeat with remaining cheese sticks. Freeze for at least 30 minutes or up to 4 hours.
4. Spray air fryer basket with cooking spray. Transfer cheese sticks into basket in a single layer. Spray sticks with cooking spray.
5. Air fry at 320°F until golden, about 3 minutes. Remove from heat and serve immediately.

BRAND SPOTLIGHT

At the intersection of Cucumber Boulevard and Vine Street, North Carolina, you'll find Mt. Olive, aka the largest independent pickle brand in the US. Mt. Olive produces over 200 million jars of pickles, peppers, and relishes annually. But when the company first started, founder Shikrey Baddour, a Lebanese immigrant, found himself in a pickle . . .

In the 1920s, Baddour and his business partner, George Moore, set out to sell brined cucumbers to nearby pickling firms. Their plan fell short, but a local business owner saw potential in Baddour's plan. He proposed the idea of working with other local business owners to establish a pickle company and pack the pickles themselves, with Moore as factory superintendent and Baddour as salesperson. Six thousand cases were produced by hand in the company's first year. Now, Mt. Olive boasts a long list of pickles and pickled foods—132 to be exact. There are twenty-three types of bread and butter pickles alone.

In 1986, the brand founded the North Carolina Pickle Festival, which includes a pickleball tournament. And every year, Mt. Olive holds a New Year's Eve pickle drop: A glowing, 3-foot-long pickle descends a flagpole as thousands of spectators watch, giving Times Square a run for its money. This New Year's Eve celebration is complete with fireworks and, of course, free pickles.

Named for its hometown of Mount Olive, North Carolina, the Mt. Olive company holds community very close to its core. No wonder they've been at it for nearly a century!

Dirty Pickletini

Serves 1

It's not a dirty martini without the olive brine. Why not rough it up by using pickle brine instead and call it a dirty pickletini? This sour, salty cocktail takes the concept of a dirty martini to the next level!

- **2 ounces London dry gin**
- **1/2 ounce pickle brine**
- **1 gherkin pickle, for garnish**

Shake liquid ingredients in a shaker tin of ice. Strain into a martini glass. Garnish with skewered gherkin.

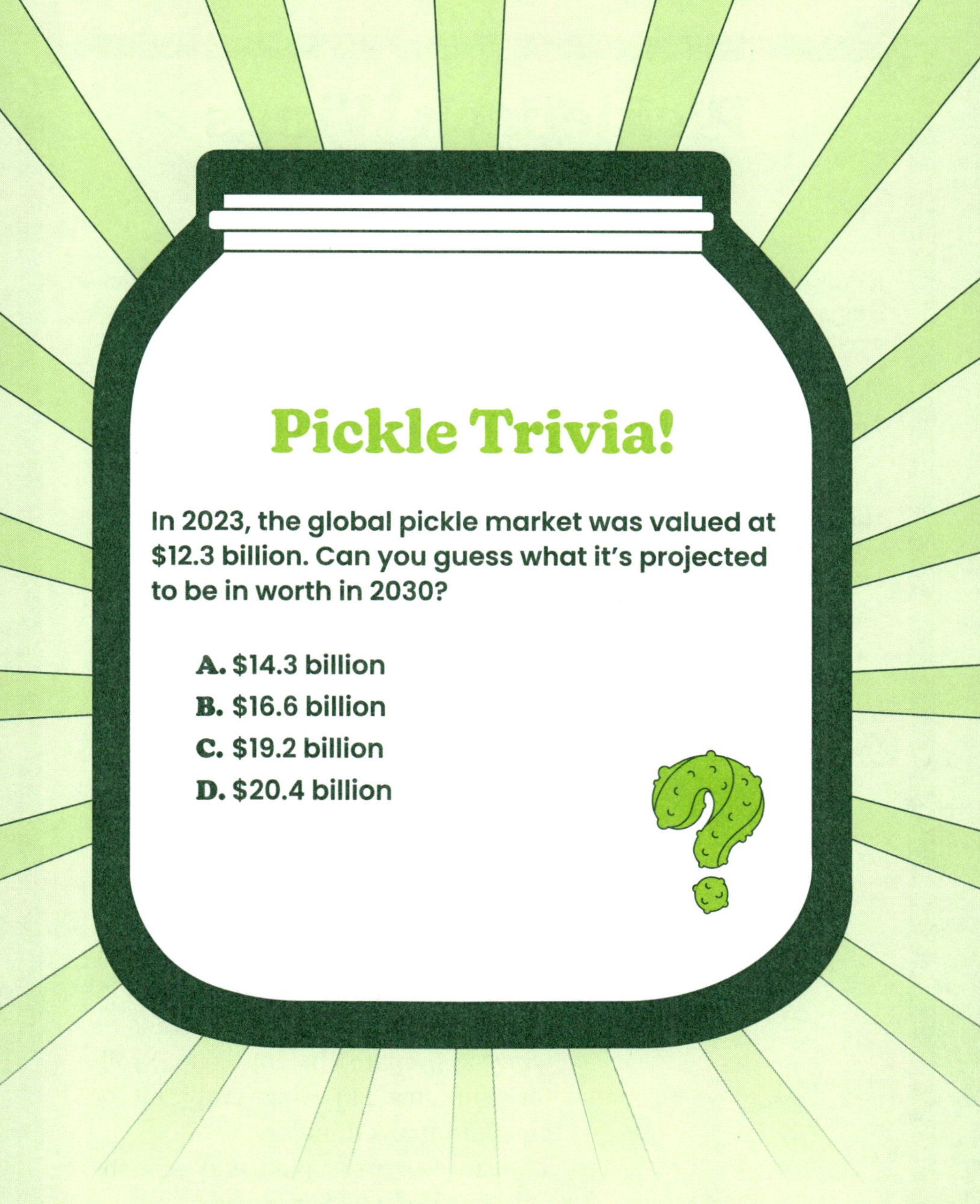

Pickle Trivia!

In 2023, the global pickle market was valued at $12.3 billion. Can you guess what it's projected to be in worth in 2030?

A. $14.3 billion

B. $16.6 billion

C. $19.2 billion

D. $20.4 billion

Answer: B. With fermented pickles gaining more popularity due to their probiotic content, the demand for pickles continues to grow higher each year.

Pickleback Wings

Serves 6

It doesn't have to be game day to enjoy this Instant Pot® favorite: chicken wings marinated in pickle juice with pickle slices on top. Sriracha, Tabasco, or whatever hot sauce you love will work beautifully with this recipe.

- 2 pounds chicken wings, cut apart at the joints
- 1 cup dill pickle brine
- 1 tablespoon packed dark brown sugar
- 1 tablespoon hot sauce
- 1/4 teaspoon garlic salt
- 1/4 teaspoon ground black pepper
- 1/2 cup bourbon whiskey
- 1 cup dill pickle slices

1. In a medium bowl, combine chicken wings and pickle brine. Refrigerate for 1 hour.
2. In a large bowl, combine brown sugar, hot sauce, garlic salt, and pepper. Set aside.
3. Add chicken wings, pickle brine, and bourbon whiskey to an Instant Pot®. Lock lid.
4. Press the Manual or Pressure Cook button and adjust time to 10 minutes. When timer beeps, let pressure release naturally for 5 minutes. Quick-release any additional pressure until float valve drops. Unlock lid.
5. Preheat broiler. Add chicken wings to spice mixture and toss. Line a baking sheet with parchment paper. Transfer wings to prepared baking sheet. Broil for 3 minutes. Flip wings and broil for an additional 3 minutes.
6. Transfer wings to a plate and garnish with pickle slices. Serve warm.

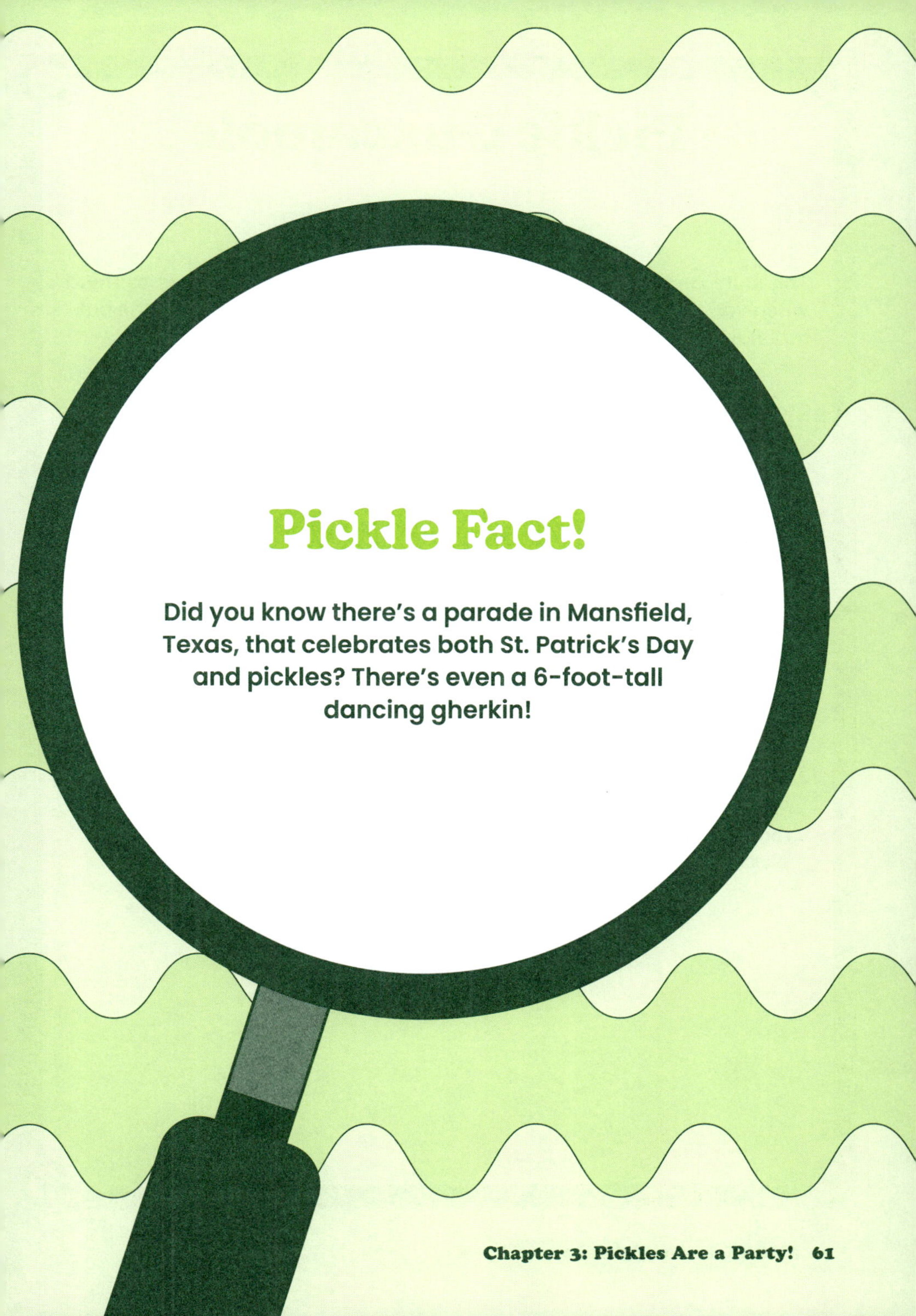

Pickle Fact!

Did you know there's a parade in Mansfield, Texas, that celebrates both St. Patrick's Day and pickles? There's even a 6-foot-tall dancing gherkin!

Pickle Guacamole

Makes 1½ cups

The salty and sour flavor of pickles may not be what comes to mind when you think of guacamole, but it pairs surprisingly well with the buttery flavor of avocado, onion, and cilantro!

2 tablespoons minced white onion
2 tablespoons chopped fresh cilantro
1 tablespoon minced jalapeño
2 teaspoons chopped fresh dill
2 tablespoons dill pickle brine
1 teaspoon fresh-squeezed lime juice
¼ teaspoon salt
2 large ripe Hass avocados
⅓ cup chopped dill pickles

1. To a medium bowl, add onion, cilantro, jalapeño, dill, pickle brine, lime juice, and salt. With a wooden spoon, gently mash ingredients five or six times until very fragrant.
2. Slice open avocados, remove pits, and scoop flesh into bowl. With a potato masher, mash until avocado is mostly smooth, with some small chunks remaining. Fold in chopped pickles. Serve immediately.

Pickle Joke!

What advice did the older pickle give to the younger pickle?

Remember to *relish* the moment!

Pickle Pops

Serves 4

Pickle pops are a fun way to use up leftover brine, and they're a perfect treat on a hot day! Taste the brine before freezing, and adjust with extra sugar if it's too tart.

8 dill pickle slices
1 cup dill pickle brine
1 tablespoon granulated sugar

1. Arrange 2 pickle slices in each popsicle mold. Set aside.
2. To a 2-cup measuring cup, add pickle brine and sugar. Whisk until sugar is dissolved. Pour brine evenly into each mold. Add sticks and lids to pops according to mold manufacturer's instructions.
3. Freeze pops for 4–6 hours, until solid. Run mold under cool running water to help pops release. Enjoy!

An Overview of Pickle Shapes

Have you ever noticed how most pickle jars don't actually say "pickles" on the label? Apparently, most pickles are identified by their *shapes* on jars—a detail that has had the internet in a frenzy in recent years. For instance, you're more likely to see "chips" or "spears" than "pickle chips" or "pickle spears." This has set off a wave of funny-but-controversial takes across social media, with many convinced that #picklesdontexist.

Bizarre conspiracy theories aside, the way pickles are shaped and textured actually plays a big role in the way brine gets absorbed and how a pickle tastes. For example, pickle chips are more tangy and intense in flavor compared to whole pickles, because the brine doesn't penetrate whole cucumbers as much as it does slices. Ultimately, that means different pickle shapes come in handy depending on how you plan to enjoy them.

The five most common pickle shapes you'll see are wholes, spears, stackers, gherkins/cornichons, and chips. While any pickle makes a great snack, whole pickles are what you seek when you're in the mood for a satisfying, ASMR-worthy crunch like no other. Whole cucumbers are for the folks who don't mind pickle juice running down their arms. Spears, meanwhile, are arguably the most versatile pickle type out there. They're great as a side dish for burgers and sandwiches, as well as a condiment for Chicago-style hot dogs.

Stackers are sliced lengthwise, making them perfect for layering on sandwiches and subs so that you get a taste of the pickle in every bite. Tiny gherkins and cornichons are great for munching on when snack cravings hit, or for making your own relish. They're also a must-have for charcuterie boards, since they offer both a flavor and texture contrast to meats, cheeses, crackers, and nuts.

Finally, pickle chips are a classic topping for burgers. They're also the perfect complement to an ice-cold soda of your choice. And whenever you order a basket of fried pickles as an appetizer for the table (or all for yourself—this is a judgment-free zone!), they're typically served as chips—making them easy to dunk in dipping sauces like blue cheese and ranch.

Pickle Fact!

Dill pickles are believed to be the most popular pickle type in the US, since they're the most versatile.

Pickleback Shot

Serves 1

You don't need to be a certified mixologist to stir up this cult favorite pickle drink. The interplay of the whiskey and the salty brine is surprisingly delicious.

1½–2 ounces whiskey
1½–2 ounces pickle brine

Pour the whiskey into one shot glass and the pickle brine into another. Take the shot of whiskey and follow it immediately with the pickle shot.

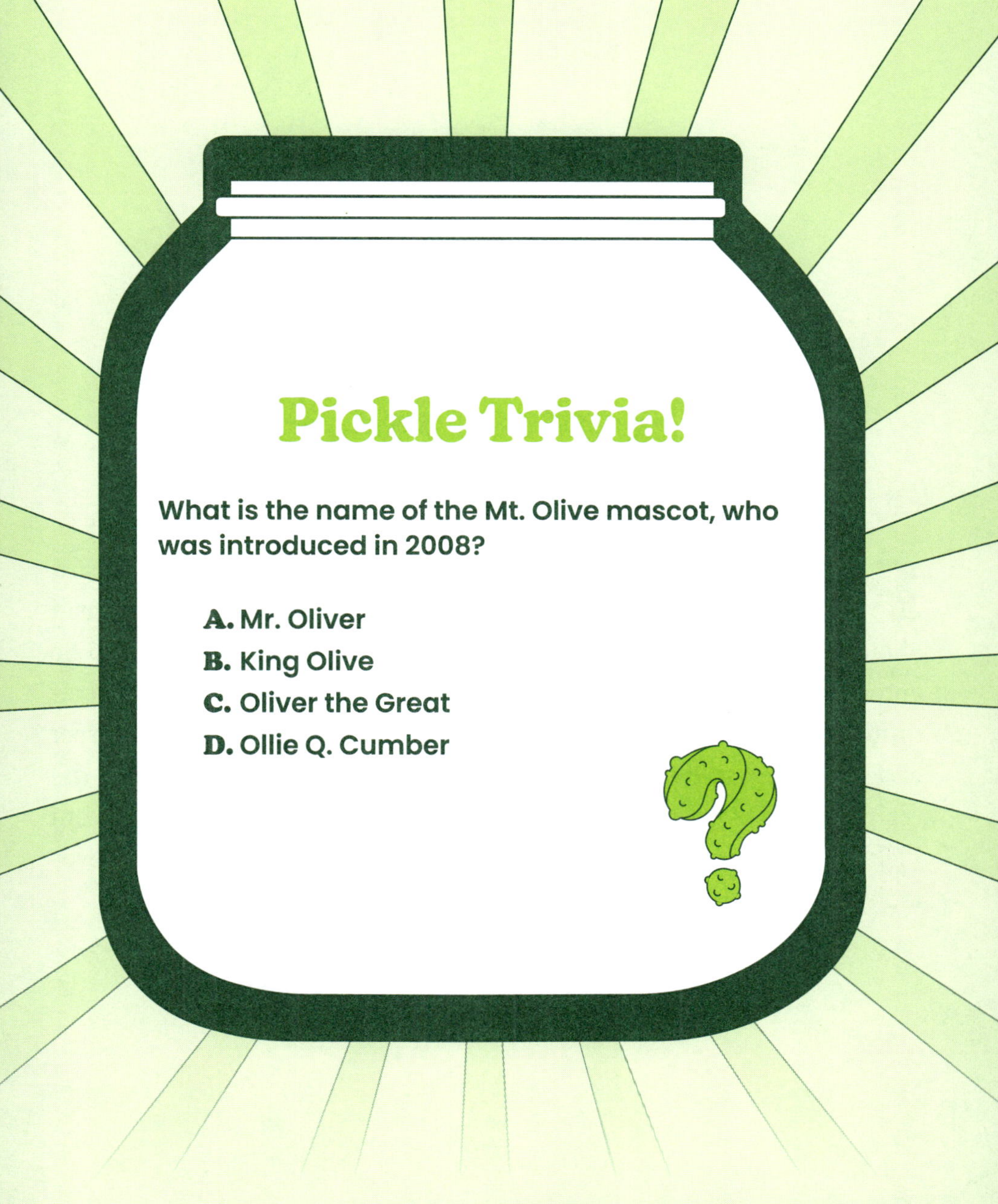

Pickle Trivia!

What is the name of the Mt. Olive mascot, who was introduced in 2008?

A. Mr. Oliver

B. King Olive

C. Oliver the Great

D. Ollie Q. Cumber

Answer: D. Mt. Olive has an entire page dedicated to Ollie Q. Cumber on its website, called "Ollie's Place." There you'll find coloring pages, puzzles, games, and more. Ollie loves rockabilly music and the Star Wars films.

CHAPTER 4

BRINE SO FINE

Pickling is a fascinating science that all pickle lovers should learn about. This chapter asks you to unleash your curiosity as you read about how raw cucumbers are transformed into pickles. You'll also be entertained by intriguing theories about how the Christmas pickle tradition came to be, as well as the story of Grillo's growing from a street cart to a brand sold in over 28,000 stores. And as a special treat, all the recipes in the pages ahead incorporate pickle brine in a major way, from Pickle-Brined Air-Fried Chicken to Dill Pickle Lemonade. You'll never look at brine the same way again!

Pickle Science

When you bite into a pickle, there's a ton of fascinating science behind every single crunch. It's *allll* about the brine! To pickle a food is to preserve it by submerging it in brine for a certain length of time. Typically, cucumber pickles are made using a vinegar-based brine, which is highly acidic, so it lowers the pH and stops harmful bacteria from thriving. Adding spices like mustard seeds and turmeric further prevents spoilage. Pickled fruits, chutneys, and relishes are often made with this same quick-process method. Ranging anywhere from a few hours to a few weeks, the quick process is the easiest and safest way to make at-home pickles.

Another common method involves soaking cucumbers in a simple saltwater brine (without vinegar). The fancy word for this process is "fermentation." Good bacteria convert the natural sugars in the cucumbers into lactic acid, and this substance does the same job that vinegar would do—it lowers the pH. (Lactic acid also makes the brine cloudy—so, in the case of fermented pickles, a cloudy brine is a good thing.) At a temperature of 70°F–75°F, fermentation can take up to three to four weeks. Full sour pickles are what you get when you wait a whole three to four weeks, while you can have half sours in as little as a week. (Kimchi and sauerkraut are also made using fermentation.)

Both methods help to preserve food, but the recipes in Chapters 6 and 7 use the quick-pickling process, so let's explore this method a little more. Making quick-process pickles often requires leaving them covered at room temperature for around twenty-four hours, but they need to be stored in the fridge after that. To make shelf-stable pickles—ones that can be kept at room temperature for years—a special process is used to sterilize everything and seal the jars. (Most of the recipes in this book don't require any of that, so before you flip to the pickle recipes in Chapters 6 and 7, make sure there's space for them in your fridge.)

Besides cucumbers, carrots, zucchini, onions, peppers, green beans, beets, and cauliflower are best for quick pickling. It's a wonderful method for getting the flavors pickle lovers desire when those cravings hit. In the fridge, quick-process pickled foods can last for a few weeks.

Even though cloudy brine is a good sign in a batch of fermented pickles, in quick-process pickles it can be a sign of yeast spoilage. Using regular table salt over pickling or canning salt can also cause a cloudy-looking brine, as can storing pickles in aluminum or copper containers. The best pickling pros use nonreactive containers (ceramic, glass, stainless steel, or Teflon) and pickling or canning salt. Typically if any cloudiness is noticed, the batch is tossed.

Pickle-Brined Air-Fried Chicken

Serves 4

The only thing more satisfying than biting into a fried chicken sandwich with a juicy, tender inside is biting into a *pickle-brined* fried chicken sandwich with a juicy, tender inside. If you prefer bite-sized, crispy nuggets, simply chop the chicken into 2-inch cubes before coating and reduce the cook time to 12 minutes.

- 4 (4-ounce) boneless, skinless chicken thighs
- ⅓ cup dill pickle brine
- 1 large egg
- 2 ounces plain pork rinds, crushed
- ½ teaspoon salt
- ¼ teaspoon ground black pepper

1. Place chicken in a large sealable bowl or bag and pour pickle brine over it. Place in refrigerator and allow to marinate for at least 1 hour, up to overnight.
2. In a small bowl, whisk egg. Place pork rinds in a separate, medium bowl.
3. Remove chicken thighs from marinade. Shake off excess pickle brine and pat thighs dry with paper towel. Sprinkle with salt and pepper.
4. Dip each thigh into egg and gently shake off excess. Press into pork rinds to coat each side. Place thighs in ungreased air fryer basket. Adjust temperature to 400°F, and cook for 20 minutes, or until golden and crispy on the outside, with an internal temperature of at least 165°F. Serve warm.

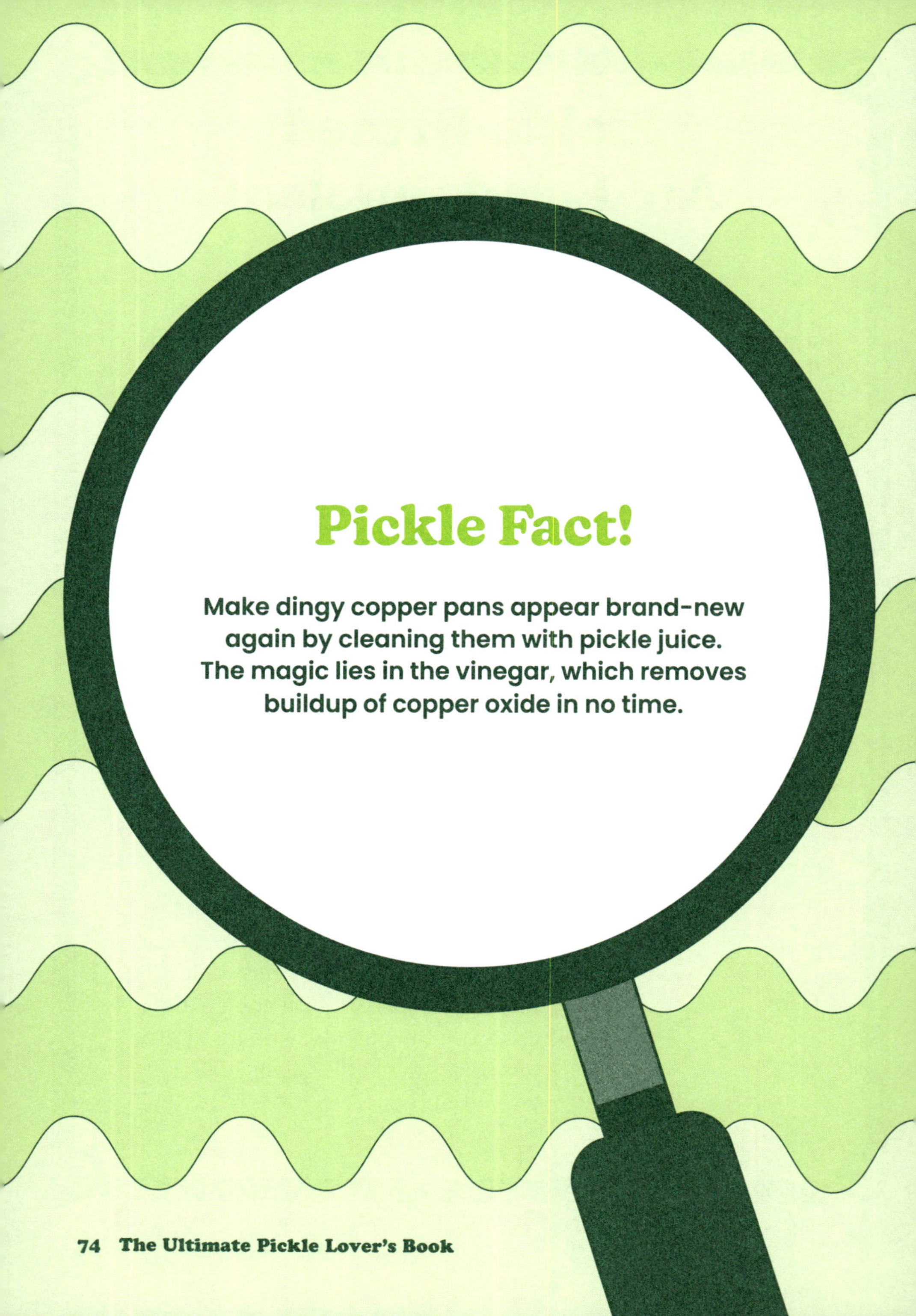

Pickle Fact!

Make dingy copper pans appear brand-new again by cleaning them with pickle juice. The magic lies in the vinegar, which removes buildup of copper oxide in no time.

Dill Pickle Lemonade

Serves 10

What's more refreshing than a cold glass of lemonade? Dill Pickle Lemonade! Share this twist on the classic with fellow pickle lovers.

4 cups water, divided
1 cup granulated sugar
1 cup fresh-squeezed lemon juice
1 cup dill pickle brine
1 medium lemon, thinly sliced
10 dill pickle spears

1. Pour 1 cup water into a medium saucepan over medium-high heat. Stir in sugar and bring to a boil, stirring until sugar is dissolved. Remove from heat and cool for 5 minutes. Transfer syrup to a large pitcher.
2. Add remaining 3 cups water, lemon juice, brine, and lemons, and stir.
3. Refrigerate for at least 2 hours.
4. Pour lemonade into tall glasses filled with ice. Garnish with pickle spears.

BRAND SPOTLIGHT

If you call yourself a Grillo's Pickles fanatic, chances are you already know that CEO Travis Grillo started his business by selling two-for-a-dollar pickle spears out of his hand-built wooden cart in downtown Boston in 2008. Rain or shine, Grillo leaned on his family's hundred-year-old recipe to grow a cult following before eventually distributing his product to over 28,000 stores nationwide.

As the company's tagline suggests, Grillo was chilling out while eating a pickle in his parents' backyard (he'd just been turned down by Nike for a job designing sneakers) when a genius idea popped into his head: "I'm going to sell these pickles."

Traditional brining or fermentation? Fermenting isn't the Grillo's way! Grillo's are quick-process pickles made with vinegar. This means they offer a fresher taste and crisper texture than fermented varieties do. Every jar also includes pickled garlic cloves for extra flavor. Beyond the taste, Grillo's is a favorite for its head-turning merch, wacky but brilliant collabs (like Grillo's toothpaste), and adorable Sam-Sam the Pickle Man logo.

The general consensus from pickle eaters across the internet is that Grillo's pickles taste a lot more like cucumbers than other brands do—a delight for anyone who prefers garden freshness to dill and salt overtones. Whether they're wholes, halves, or chips, or sweet, spicy, or sour, Grillo's has been making people fall in love with pickles for years!

Creamy Pickle Vinaigrette

Makes ¾ cup

Don't let leftover pickle brine go to waste! You can use it to make a pickle-infused salad dressing that is creamy, sharp, and perfect for dressing salad greens or pasta or drizzling over grilled chicken or seafood. You can also use bread and butter brine in this recipe—just omit the sugar.

¼ cup extra-virgin olive oil

¼ cup dill pickle brine

3 tablespoons mayonnaise

1 tablespoon Dijon mustard

1 tablespoon chopped fresh dill

2 teaspoons granulated sugar

¼ teaspoon ground black pepper

Add all ingredients to a medium bowl and whisk to combine. Use immediately, or refrigerate for up to 5 days. Whisk well before serving.

In 2000, which team did the Philadelphia Eagles defeat while drinking jugs of ice-cold pickle juice throughout the game?

A. New England Patriots

B. Chicago Bears

C. San Francisco 49ers

D. Dallas Cowboys

Answer: D. On September 3, 2000, the Eagles defeated the Cowboys in sweltering heat—109°F, to be exact! The team credited pickle juice for keeping them hydrated and staving off muscle cramps.

Vodka Picklet

Serves 1

Cucumber pickles plus citrus fruit equals one stellar cocktail. The acidity in the citrus is mirrored and complemented by the acidity in the brine.

- **1½ ounces vodka**
- **½ ounce Rose's sweetened lime juice (or ¼ ounce fresh-squeezed lime juice and ¼ ounce simple syrup)**
- **½ ounce pickle brine**
- **1 lime wedge, for garnish**
- **2 pickle slices, for garnish**

Add all liquid ingredients to a shaker tin half filled with ice. Shake and strain into a rocks glass of ice. Garnish with lime wedge and pickle slices.

HA HA

Pickle Joke!

What do you call a genius pickle?

A *brine*-iac.

HA HA

HA

The Christmas Pickle Tradition

A pickle may seem like the most unlikely Christmas tree ornament . . . but this isn't the case in the midwestern US, especially Michigan. Merrymakers there place a pickle-shaped ornament last on the Christmas tree when it's being decorated. Then, the first person to spot the pickle on the tree on Christmas Day opens the first gift or receives a special treat. In some cultures, it's also a sign that that person will have good luck for the year ahead.

Germany is credited as the origin of this fun tradition; however, the vast majority of Germans have never heard of it. So, who can you thank for the Christmas pickle? It's an open question with a few possible answers. In one theory, a German American soldier during the Civil War is believed to have been starving on Christmas Eve; he begged a guard for a pickle. Because the pickle helped the soldier live on, he was inspired to hang a pickle on his Christmas tree upon returning home to his family.

Another theory is thought to be far less likely, but you can be the judge. Two boys are said to have been traveling home from boarding school for Christmas. They decided to rest at an inn for the night, only to meet a wicked innkeeper who supposedly trapped them inside a pickle barrel. That evening, Santa Claus stopped by the inn and freed the boys from the barrel.

In a third theory, someone hawking German glass ornaments invented the so-called tradition of the Christmas pickle with the hope of boosting sales across American stores. For what it's worth, Tim Merck, the founder of the family-owned Old World Christmas, imported his ornaments from Germany to the US. Their pickle ornament remains the company's bestselling ornament, and the Christmas pickle tradition's origin "story" still gets printed on every single ornament box.

No matter which tale you choose to believe, hanging a pickle ornament is a beloved tradition for many!

Kool-Aid Pickles

Serves 8

These colorful treats originated in Mississippi and can be made with any flavor of Kool-Aid you like! They make a tasty snack on their own, but they're also delicious as a side to fried and smoked foods.

- **1 (32-ounce) jar dill pickle spears**
- **½ cup granulated sugar**
- **1 (0.22-ounce) packet Kool-Aid drink mix, any flavor**

1. Drain pickle brine into a medium bowl, leaving pickle spears in jar.
2. Add sugar and Kool-Aid mix to pickle brine. Whisk until dissolved.
3. Carefully pour brine mixture back into jar until it covers pickles. There will be extra brine. Cover jar with lid and refrigerate for 5 days before enjoying.

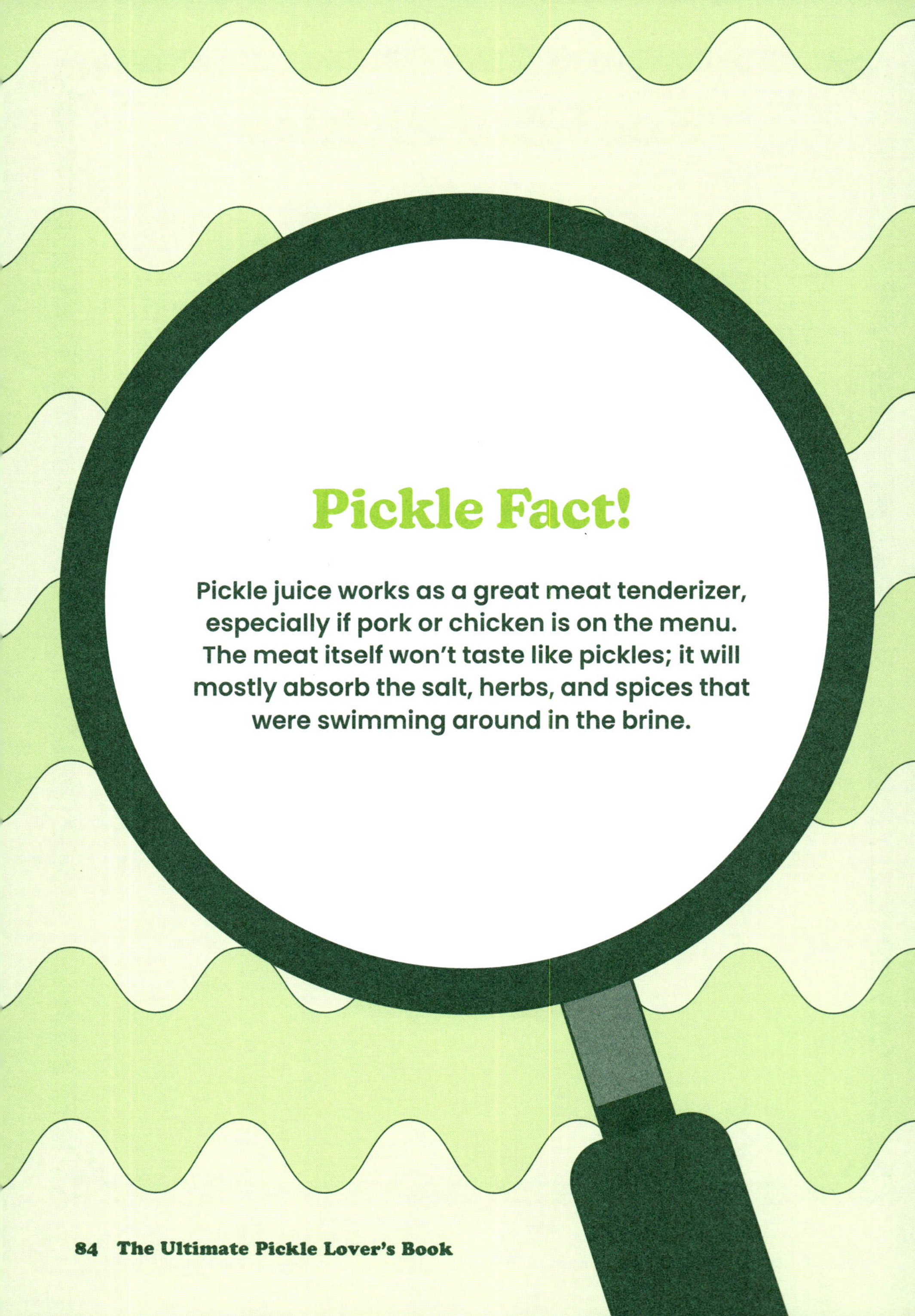

Pickle Fact!

Pickle juice works as a great meat tenderizer, especially if pork or chicken is on the menu. The meat itself won't taste like pickles; it will mostly absorb the salt, herbs, and spices that were swimming around in the brine.

Pickle-y Hot Sauce

Makes 2 cups

This sauce packs a punch of heat and a zippy tang from blended-in dill pickles and pickle brine. If the sauce is too thick to blend easily, feel free to add more pickle brine or water, 2–3 tablespoons at a time, until it loosens.

- 3 large jalapeños, stems and seeds removed
- 3 medium tomatoes, stems removed, quartered
- 2 tablespoons vegetable oil
- ½ cup dill pickle slices
- ½ cup dill pickle brine
- 1 teaspoon chopped fresh dill
- ¼ teaspoon garlic powder
- ¼ teaspoon onion powder

1. Preheat oven to 400°F and line a baking sheet with aluminum foil.
2. To baking sheet, add jalapeños and tomatoes. Add oil and toss to coat evenly. Bake for 20–30 minutes, until vegetables are tender and lightly charred.
3. Transfer hot vegetables to blender with remaining ingredients, and purée on high for 1 minute. Scrape down sides, and purée again for 30–45 seconds, until sauce is smooth.
4. Place a strainer over a large bowl, and line it with cheesecloth or a coffee filter. Slowly pour sauce through strainer, then transfer strained sauce to a clean bottle. Store in refrigerator for up to 2 weeks.

Pickle Trivia!

Brine isn't just made for chugging! It can be repurposed in some pretty surprising ways. But which is *not* a recommended use for brine?

A. Lowering the pH level of soil

B. Boosting compost piles

C. Making dull hardwood floors shine again

D. Salting icy roads

Answer: C. Brine that's been significantly diluted can be poured directly into soil, helping plants to grow and making hydrangeas more vibrant. In addition to offering a nutritional boost to compost piles, brine is a pretty common alternative to rock salt on roads in many states. But one thing brine cannot do? Shine hardwood floors. In fact, brine can ruin the finish of beautiful hardwood floors.

Pickle Bloody Mary

Serves 2

Spicy, tangy, and infused with pickle brine, this drink is a pickle twist on the brunch classic! Pickle brine intensity can vary by brand, so feel free to add a few extra teaspoons if desired. You can also make this alcohol-free by omitting the vodka.

- 1 teaspoon celery salt
- 1/4 teaspoon Tajín
- 1/4 teaspoon ground black pepper
- 1 lemon wedge
- 2 cups V8 Vegetable Juice
- 2 ounces vodka
- 2 tablespoons dill pickle brine
- 1 tablespoon fresh-squeezed lemon juice
- 2 dashes Worcestershire sauce
- 2 dashes hot pepper sauce
- 2 dill pickle spears
- 2 celery stalks with leaves
- 2 sprigs fresh dill

1. On a small plate, combine celery salt, Tajín, and pepper.
2. Rub rims of cocktail glasses with lemon wedge, then roll in prepared seasoning. Fill glasses with ice cubes and set aside.
3. In a pitcher, combine vegetable juice, vodka, pickle brine, lemon juice, Worcestershire sauce, and hot pepper sauce. Divide between glasses. Garnish with pickle, celery, and dill. Serve immediately.

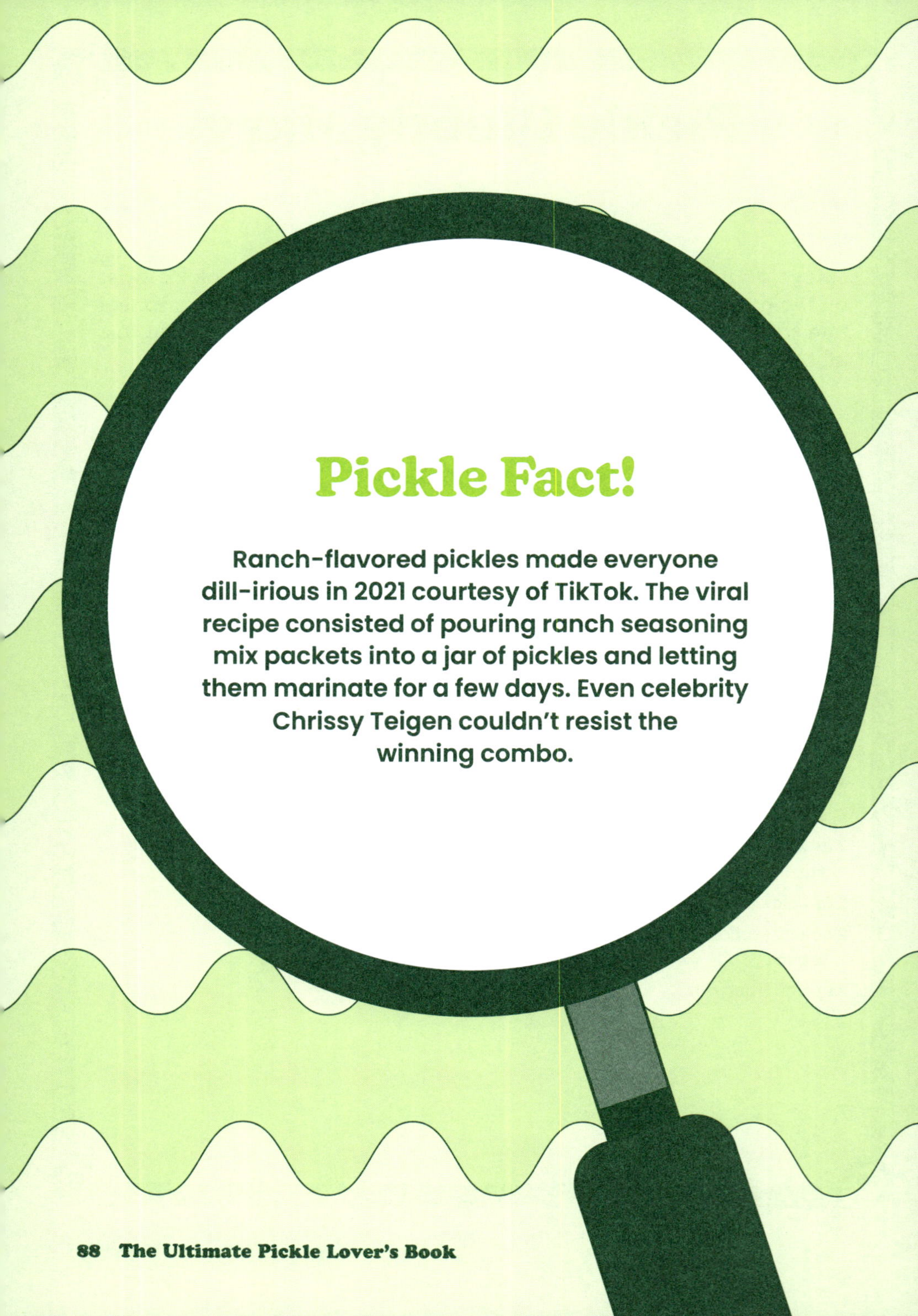

Pickle Fact!

Ranch-flavored pickles made everyone dill-irious in 2021 courtesy of TikTok. The viral recipe consisted of pouring ranch seasoning mix packets into a jar of pickles and letting them marinate for a few days. Even celebrity Chrissy Teigen couldn't resist the winning combo.

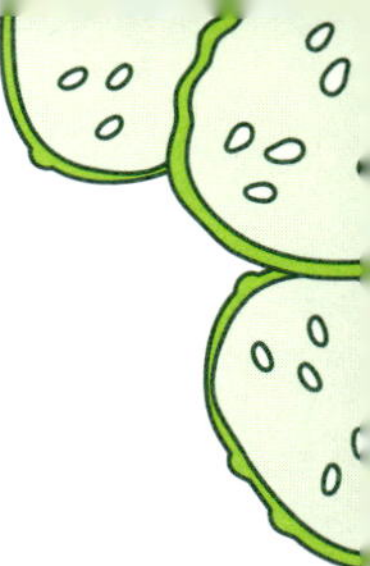

CHAPTER 5

PICKLED POP CULTURE

From viral food trends to notable appearances across TV and movies, pickles have a briny way of stealing the show. In this chapter, you'll witness firsthand how pickles have grabbed viewers' attention over the years. The following pages put the spotlight on the A-listers who live for pickles, as well as recipes highlighting the versatility of the wonderful briny treat. Here you'll encounter Pickle Cupcakes and Pickle-in-a-Blanket, and you'll meet Claus Claussen, the man behind the trusted brand that's been beloved for over a century. Get ready to dive into all the ways that pickles make the director's cut!

Pickles on Screen

Do scenes like Bridget Jones's mother serving gherkins on toothpicks at an ugly sweater party or Susan Sarandon's character in *The Witches of Eastwick* eating pickles while grocery shopping live rent-free in your mind? So will these other dill-tastic moments:

- ***Rugrats.*** Calling all nineties kids! If you're a millennial, you may have fond memories of Tommy, Chuckie, Phil, Lil, Angelica, Susie, and Cynthia, but you may have forgotten that protagonist Tommy's last name was (drumroll, please!) Pickles. And his baby brother's name was (wait for it) Dil. *Rugrats* cocreator Paul Germain said the last name Pickles "just occurred" to him and didn't have any hidden meaning. Still, fans like to imagine it's a hint that Tommy and Dil grew up to become pickle-obsessed.
- ***Jersey Shore.*** Cast member Snooki's pickle adoration was no secret; she even went so far as to drink brine straight from the jar in one episode. And the momentous scene where Snooki ate fried pickles for the first time is a fan favorite.
- ***Rick and Morty.*** The next time you want to skip family therapy or anything even mildly unpleasant, why not transform yourself into a pickle, just like genius scientist Rick Sanchez from *Rick and Morty*? Known as Pickle Rick, this tangy, crunchy version of Mr. Sanchez became a cultural phenomenon in 2017. Pickle Rick was so popular that he got his own board game, Funko Pop! figures, Pringles flavor, and breakfast cereal. Long live Pickle Rick. (Oh, and there's no real Russian myth about Solenya the Pickle Man, though *solenya* is the Russian word for "pickles.")

- ***Friends.*** You're an *extremely* observant viewer if you've ever peeped the "Homemade Pickles" crock sitting on the kitchen counter in Monica and Rachel's apartment on *Friends*. But if you have, you aren't the only one; countless viewers have noticed that crock, inspiring replicas across Amazon and Etsy.
- ***Portlandia.*** Band-Aids? Broken shoe heels? Empty CD cases? Parking tickets? Nickels? You can pickle that! Just ask Bryce Shivers and Lisa Eversman. In one sketch on the popular show *Portlandia*, this couple proves they can pickle pretty much anything.

Chamoy Pickles

Serves 8

With origins in Mexico, the chamoy pickle is a part of the TikTok viral food hall of fame! Dill pickles are soaked in chamoy, a pickled fruit condiment, then dressed up with chips, fruit snacks, and tangy tamarind.

- **1 (32-ounce) jar whole dill pickles (about 8 pickles)**
- **1 (32-ounce) bottle chamoy**
- **1 (3.25-ounce) bag Takis chips**
- **1 (0.85-ounce) bag Lucas Skwinkles**
- **1 (1.26-ounce) container tamarind-flavored Lucas Gusano**
- **8 (0.5-ounce) rolls Fruit Roll-Ups**

1. Drain all but ⅓ cup brine out of the pickle jar. Pour in enough chamoy to cover pickles. Close jar with lid, and shake to combine. Refrigerate for 5 days.
2. To assemble, remove pickles from jar and cut ½" off tip of each. Scoop out inside of each pickle with a small spoon.
3. Stuff center of each pickle with Takis and Skwinkles, and drizzle with Gusano. Wrap each pickle in 1 Fruit Roll-Up. Serve immediately.

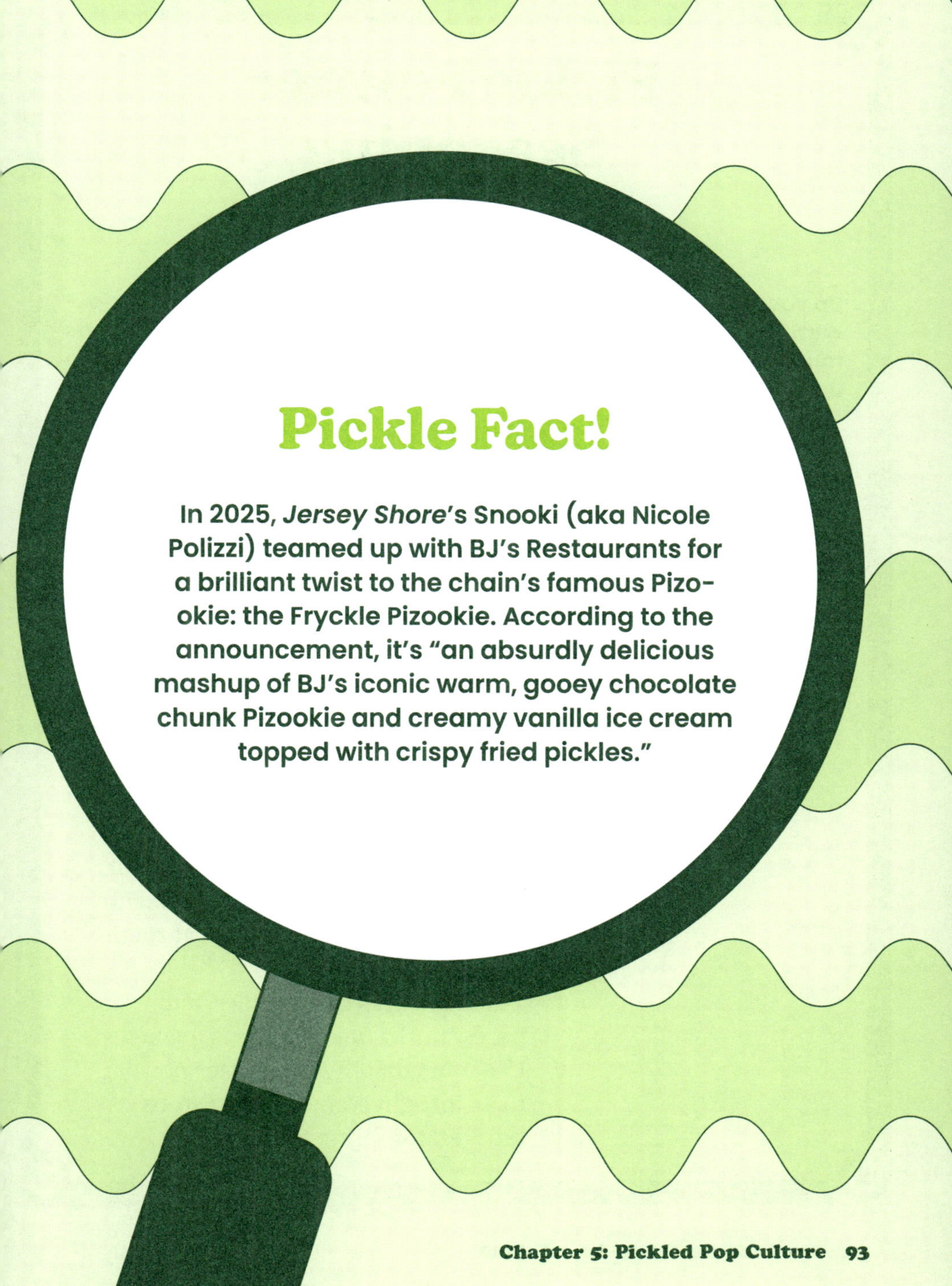

Pickle Fact!

In 2025, *Jersey Shore*'s Snooki (aka Nicole Polizzi) teamed up with BJ's Restaurants for a brilliant twist to the chain's famous Pizookie: the Fryckle Pizookie. According to the announcement, it's "an absurdly delicious mashup of BJ's iconic warm, gooey chocolate chunk Pizookie and creamy vanilla ice cream topped with crispy fried pickles."

Pickle Powder Seasoning

Makes ¾ cup

Do you love dill pickle popcorn? Are you a fan of pickle-flavored chips? With this seasoning powder, you can make your own dishes with as much pickle goodness as you like! If you have a dehydrator, you can use it here. Set it to 130°F for 8–16 hours.

1 pound dill pickles

1. Preheat oven to 175°F and line a baking sheet with parchment paper.
2. With a mandoline set to ⅛" thickness (or the thinnest setting that allows for even slices), slice pickles. Transfer slices to a large bowl filled with cool water and let pickles soak for 20 minutes. Once soaked, strain slices and lay on a tray lined with paper towels. With more towels, pat tops to absorb excess liquid.
3. Arrange slices on prepared baking sheet, and bake in an even layer for 3–4 hours, flipping slices every hour, until slices are crisp and snap cleanly when broken. Let slices cool at room temperature for 1 hour.
4. Transfer slices to a blender, and purée until a fine powder is formed. Use immediately, or transfer powder to an airtight container and store in refrigerator for up to 4 weeks.

BRAND SPOTLIGHT

What does a vegetable farmer from Germany residing in Chicago do when he has a bunch of leftover cucumbers that he cannot sell? Pickle them! Founder Claus Claussen's light-bulb moment in 1870 marked the start of a company that's still going strong more than 150 years later. Many decades after the company's founding, in the 1960s, Claus's great-grandson Ed Claussen developed Claussen's first refrigerated pickle, a big step toward the Claussen formula that so many have come to know and love today.

Claussen cucumbers are pickled almost immediately after they're harvested—in ten days or less! Additionally, Claussen's pickles are never heated or pasteurized, so they're packed fresh—making the crunch unbeatable. It's why you will find them refrigerated and not on the shelf with the rest of the pickle brands. Bravo if you've seen the "cold, crisp, Claussen" ad from 1992 showing Claussen pickles snapping clean in half when bent.

For Claussen loyalists, Claussen is one of the few national brands that come close to farmers' market–style pickles in terms of crunch and freshness. With Claussen, you won't find a million varieties, but instead a few delicious staples: Kosher Dill, Sweet Bread 'N Butter, Hot & Spicy, and Hearty Garlic. And you can bet they come in spears, chips, slices, halves, and wholes. There's even a taste tester whose job is to sample the spicy brine used in Claussen's spicy pickles to make sure it has enough heat.

In recent years, Claussen has released a pickle-flavored sparkling wine cocktail, as well as pickle-flavored jelly beans—proof that the tried-and-true brand isn't afraid to move with the times.

Chickle

Serves 1

This cheesy, tangy snack is perfect for pickle lovers *and* cheese lovers. The key is to start with a lightly greased nonstick skillet that is hot before adding the cheese. You want it to get very crusty and brown before wrapping it around the pickle!

- 1 (1-ounce) slice low-moisture mozzarella cheese
- 1 dill pickle spear, patted dry

1. Heat an 8" nonstick skillet, lightly sprayed with nonstick cooking spray, over medium heat until hot, about 3 minutes. Add cheese slice and cook until cheese is golden around the edges and bubbling, about 5 minutes.
2. Add pickle in center of cheese, and use a spatula to wrap cheese around pickle. If cheese does not easily release from pan, cook for 30–45 seconds more. Transfer wrapped pickle to a paper towel–lined plate. Let cool for 2 minutes, then serve.

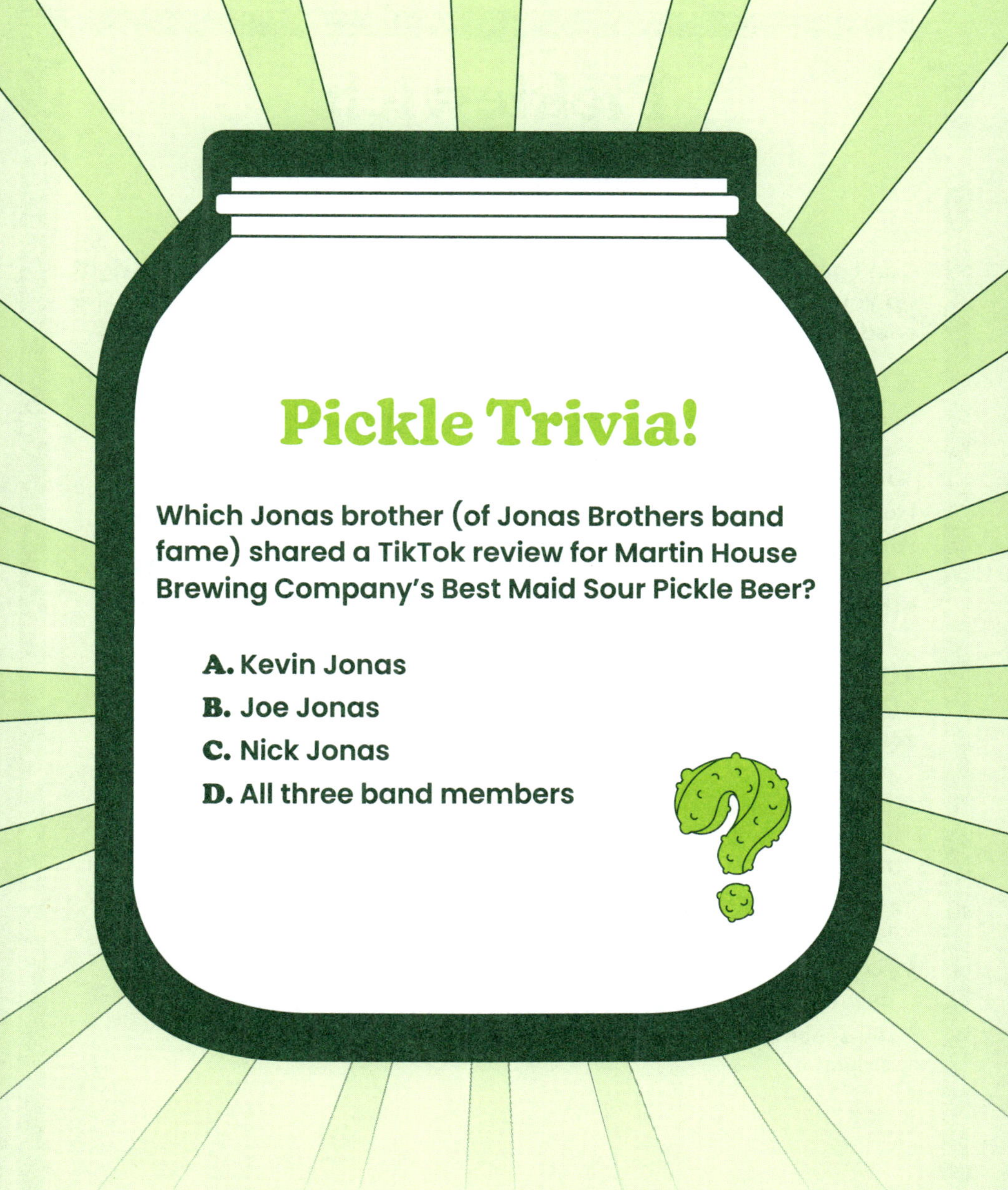

Pickle Trivia!

Which Jonas brother (of Jonas Brothers band fame) shared a TikTok review for Martin House Brewing Company's Best Maid Sour Pickle Beer?

A. Kevin Jonas

B. Joe Jonas

C. Nick Jonas

D. All three band members

Answer: C. Nick Jonas gave the pickled-infused beer a 7 out of 10, calling it "pretty pickle forward."

Picklewich

Serves 1

Can't get enough pickles on your favorite deli sub? This sandwich is right up your alley! This sub swaps bread for an extra-large pickle with the seeds scooped out and stuffed with cheese, meats, and fresh veggies.

- **1 extra-large dill pickle, sliced in half, seeds removed**
- **1 tablespoon mayonnaise**
- **1 tablespoon deli mustard**
- **2 (1-ounce) slices provolone cheese**
- **3 (1-ounce) slices turkey**
- **3 (1-ounce) slices ham**
- **3 (1-ounce) slices hard salami**
- **1 (1/4") slice from a large tomato, cut into half-moons**
- **1/2 cup shredded iceberg lettuce**
- **1/4 cup thinly sliced red onion**
- **1/2 teaspoon dried oregano**

Lay pickle halves, cut sides up, on a work surface. Pat cut sides of pickle with paper towel to remove excess moisture. Spread mayonnaise on one side and mustard on the other. On one half of pickle, layer on cheese, turkey, ham, salami, tomato, lettuce, and onion. Sprinkle oregano evenly over top. Top with other half of pickle. Serve immediately.

Pickle Joke!

What's a baby gherkin's favorite TV channel?

Pickleodeon.

Fried Pickle Dip

Serves 8

This recipe takes all the best flavors and textures of fried pickles—the toasty coating, the creamy ranch dip, and the tangy pickles—and transforms them into an irresistible dip! It pairs well with your favorite chips and crackers. Don't skip the chilling time, which allows the flavors to develop.

- 2 cups sour cream
- 4 ounces cream cheese (at room temperature)
- 1 (0.4-ounce) packet Hidden Valley Ranch Restaurant-Style Dressing & Recipe Mix
- 2 tablespoons dill pickle brine
- 1 tablespoon chopped fresh dill
- 1 tablespoon chopped fresh chives
- 1/2 teaspoon onion powder
- 1/4 teaspoon garlic powder
- 1 1/4 cups finely chopped dill pickles
- 1 cup panko
- 5 tablespoons unsalted butter, melted

1. To a large bowl, add sour cream and cream cheese. With a hand mixer, beat on low speed until mixture is just combined, about 30 seconds. Increase speed to medium and beat until mixture is smooth, about 2 minutes.
2. Add remaining ingredients up to garlic powder, and beat on low speed for 30 seconds, or until all spices are well blended. Add pickles and fold to mix. Cover and refrigerate for at least 4 hours.
3. Just before serving, prepare topping. In a medium bowl, combine panko and butter, and mix until evenly combined. Heat a 10" skillet over medium heat. Add panko mixture and cook, stirring often, until mixture is golden brown, about 5 minutes. Remove from heat and set aside to cool.
4. Transfer dip to a serving dish and top with toasted panko. Serve immediately.

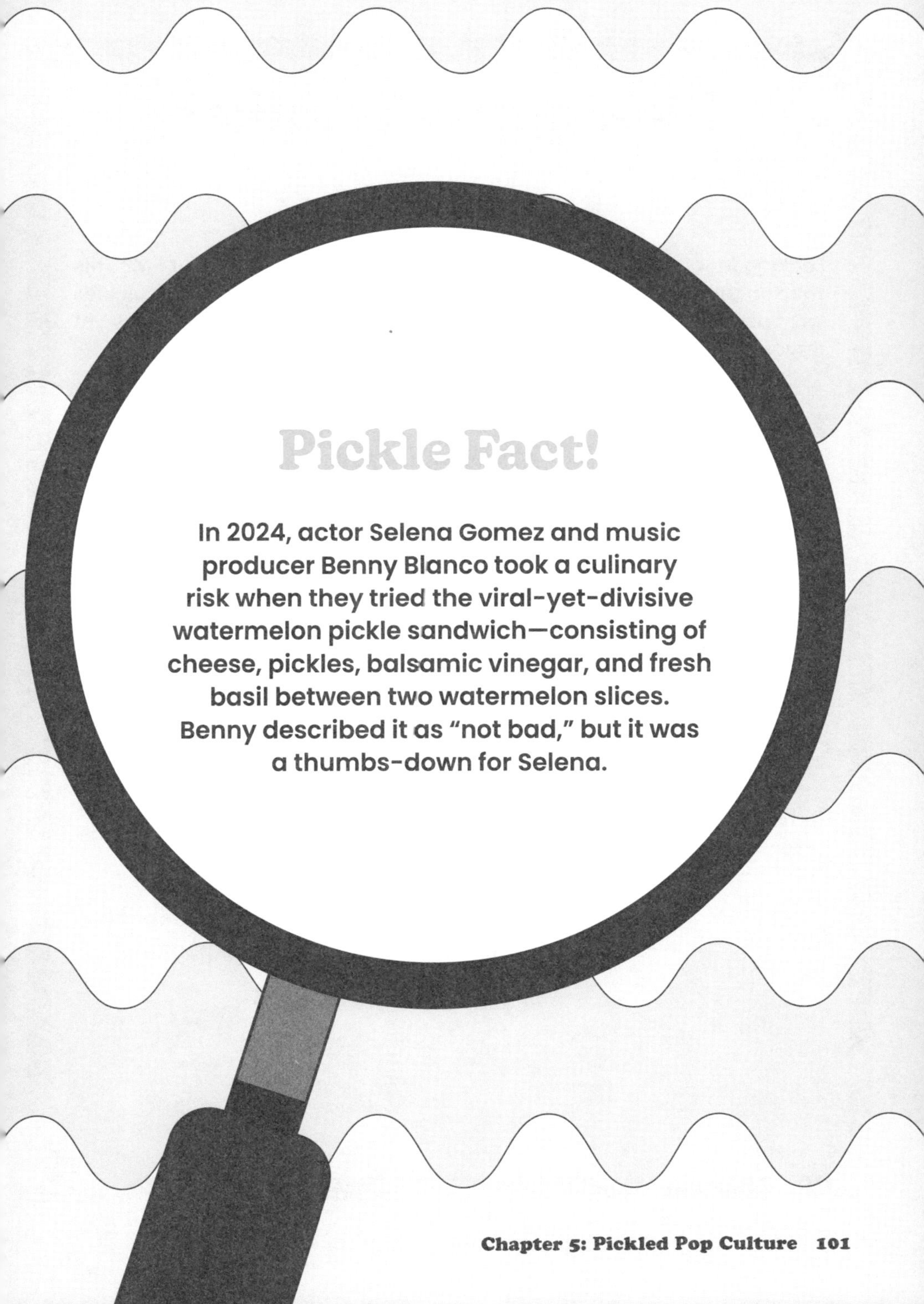

Pickle Fact!

In 2024, actor Selena Gomez and music producer Benny Blanco took a culinary risk when they tried the viral-yet-divisive watermelon pickle sandwich—consisting of cheese, pickles, balsamic vinegar, and fresh basil between two watermelon slices. Benny described it as "not bad," but it was a thumbs-down for Selena.

Pickle-in-a-Blanket

Serves 8

Looking for a fun snack for the pickle-obsessed person in your life? This take on the pig in a blanket tosses the hot dogs in favor of tangy pickles wrapped with savory ham and cheese in crescent dough for an easy yet flavor-packed dish everyone will love!

2 ounces cream cheese (at room temperature)

½ cup shredded sharp Cheddar cheese

1 (8-ounce) can crescent roll dough

4 (0.5-ounce) slices deli ham, cut into half-moons, patted dry

4 dill pickle spears, cut in half crosswise and patted dry

2 tablespoons unsalted butter, melted

¼ teaspoon garlic powder

1. Preheat oven to 375°F and line a baking sheet with parchment paper.
2. In a small bowl, beat cream cheese with a spatula until smooth, then add Cheddar and mix until well combined.
3. On a work surface, unroll crescent roll dough and separate into triangles. Divide cheese mixture among triangles and spread so each triangle is evenly coated. Top each with a slice of ham. Lay a pickle spear along wider edge of each triangle and roll up.
4. Transfer rolls onto prepared baking sheet. Brush each with butter and sprinkle with garlic powder. Bake for 15–18 minutes, until rolls are baked and golden brown. Cool on pan for 5 minutes before serving.

Celeb Pickle Snacks

Stars—they're just like us! Every so often, they can't resist the urge to chug down a jar of pickle juice. It's safe to say that pickles have a briny spot in these celebrities' hearts:

- Elvis Presley's love of peanut butter, banana, and bacon sandwiches might get all the glory, but he also had a weakness for pickles—*deep fried pickles*, that is.
- In Vancouver, musician Harry Styles declared Hobbs Pickles as his favorite, saying the gourmet food spot served the "most delicious pickle" he'd ever had. And at one of the shows during his Love On Tour, a fan held up a sign asking, "Do you like pickles?"—to which he responded, "I *do* like pickles."
- In 2025, actor Pamela Anderson teased her own pickle brand. Turns out she grew up making pickles. In fact, her great aunt won awards for them on Vancouver Island. She even experiments with unusual pickle flavors, adding dried rose petals for a floral vibe.
- Who could forget singer Dua Lipa's polarizing Diet Coke "cocktail" that took over the internet in 2024? While enjoying BBQ with her friends, she paused for a moment to pour Diet Coke over crushed ice. No big dill, right? Well, things took an interesting turn when she added pickle juice and jalapeño juice. She then added some sliced pickles and jalapeños as garnish. Don't knock it 'til you've tried it!

- Actor-singer Demi Lovato loves pickles so much that she was gifted a collection of pickles for her birthday. And for National Pickle Day she shared a video of herself whipping up lots of briny dishes, including cheesy pickle waffles. She even has a dog named Pickle.
- Actor Matthew McConaughey has declared himself a pickle expert. He and celebrity chef Nick DiGiovanni created a viral pickle margarita, mixing the drink right in a jar of dills.
- From pouring pickle juice on popcorn for an extra zing to devouring pickle-flavored snow cones, actor Selena Gomez's fondness for pickles might be unmatched. She even combines pickles with Reese's Peanut Butter Cups. On Valentine's Day of 2024, her then-fiancé, Benny Blanco, made her fried pickles.
- Adam Sandler is iconic for a lot of reasons, from his acting credits to his produced hits. But photos of him walking around New York City while eating pickles straight from the jar will forever be cherished by fellow pickle enthusiasts.

Pickle Margarita

Serves 1

This surprisingly complex margarita has just the right mix of sweet, tangy, and salty, with a hint of herby dill. While a salt rim on the glass is traditional, why not mix in a little Pickle Powder Seasoning or swap the salt for Tajín for a kick?

1½ ounces white tequila
1½ ounces triple sec
3 ounces sour mix
½ ounce dill pickle brine
½ ounce fresh-squeezed lime juice
1 dill pickle slice

Mix all liquid ingredients together and serve in a salt-rimmed glass filled with ice. Garnish with pickle slice.

Pickle Cupcakes

Makes 12 Cupcakes

This recipe uses naturally sweet bread and butter pickle brine for a sweet and savory flavor. The cupcakes are topped with silky cream cheese frosting and a bit of pickle for a fun garnish!

For Cupcakes

- 1½ cups all-purpose flour
- ⅔ cup granulated sugar
- 1¼ teaspoons baking powder
- ¼ teaspoon baking soda
- ⅛ teaspoon salt
- ½ cup vegetable oil
- ½ cup sour cream
- 2 large eggs
- ¼ cup bread and butter pickle brine

For Frosting

- 8 ounces cream cheese (at room temperature)
- ½ cup unsalted butter (at room temperature)
- 2 cups confectioners' sugar
- 1 tablespoon heavy cream
- ¼ teaspoon pure vanilla extract
- 2 tablespoons green sprinkles
- 3 bread and butter pickle chips, quartered

1. Preheat oven to 350°F and line a 12-cup muffin pan with paper cupcake liners.
2. To a medium bowl, add flour, sugar, baking powder, baking soda, and salt. Whisk well to combine.
3. To a separate medium bowl, add oil, sour cream, eggs, and pickle brine. Whisk until fully combined. Pour wet ingredients into dry ingredients and mix with a spatula until just combined, about 15 strokes. Batter should be relatively smooth, with a few small lumps. No dry flour should remain.

4. Divide batter among cupcake liners. Bake for 20–25 minutes, until cupcakes are golden brown and puffed and spring back when centers are gently pressed. Let cool in pan for 3 minutes, then transfer to a wire rack to cool completely.
5. Once cupcakes are cool, prepare frosting. Add cream cheese and butter to a large bowl. With a hand mixer on low speed, beat until fully combined. Add confectioners' sugar, cream, and vanilla, and beat on low speed for 30 seconds, then increase speed to medium and beat for 30–45 seconds more, until mixture is smooth.
6. Spread or pipe frosting on cupcakes. Sprinkle with green sprinkles, and top each with a piece of pickle. Serve immediately, or place in an airtight container and refrigerate for up to 4 days.

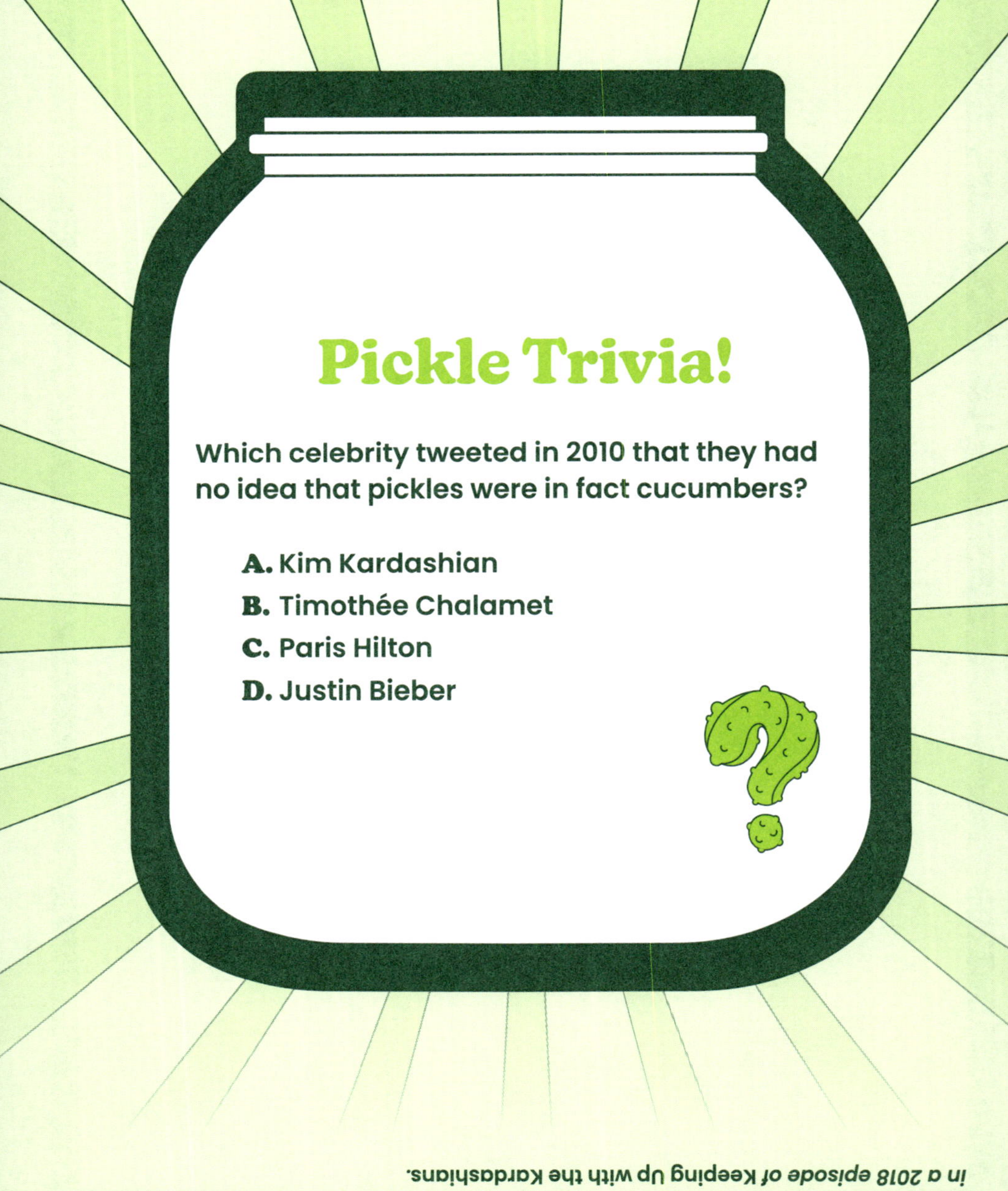

Pickle Trivia!

Which celebrity tweeted in 2010 that they had no idea that pickles were in fact cucumbers?

A. Kim Kardashian

B. Timothée Chalamet

C. Paris Hilton

D. Justin Bieber

Answer: A. Turns out Kim Kardashian is still a little confused over whether pickles are made from cucumbers. "I still don't even know, and I don't care to research," she said in a 2018 episode of Keeping Up with the Kardashians.

BECOME A PICKLE GENIUS

Why settle for being a pickle expert when you can become a pickle genius? This part is all about taking your pickle obsession to new heights. Here you'll learn the basics of making your own quick-process pickles, which are a great way to create the flavor of your briny favorites in less than twenty-four hours. As you flip through the pages ahead, you'll find recipes for both cucumber and non-cucumber pickles. While you're at it, you'll familiarize yourself with the history of pickling and what it looks like across different cultures. Let's brine!

CHAPTER 6

PICKLING 101

Pickles boast an impressive fan club through history! Cleopatra, Julius Caesar, Aristotle, and more sung their praises. In this chapter, not only do you get to bite deeper into the history of pickling, including the surprising ways pickles were utilized thousands of years ago; you also get to explore recipes for quick and easy refrigerator pickles, including dill, bread and butter, half sour, and more. Then, you'll move on to growing your own spices and herbs for top-tier homemade pickles. Last but not least, you'll find out why Dietz & Watson might be the hidden gem of pickles.

The History of Pickling

Pickles have become more and more trendy in recent years, but they're nothing new. Born out of a need to preserve foods for long voyages and prevent scurvy outbreaks among sailors on tightly packed ships, they have come a long way since being consumed solely for the purpose of convenience or staving off diseases.

Pickles as a concept date all the way back to ancient Mesopotamia (present-day Iraq), around 2400 B.C.E. (That's over 4,400 years ago!) Scientists believe that cucumbers originated in India, specifically in the foothills of the Himalayas, and were brought to Mesopotamia, where people began preserving them using brine or vinegar.

Eventually, pickles made their way to the Western Hemisphere, where Italian explorer Amerigo Vespucci, the namesake of America, sold pickled vegetables and meats to other explorers, including Christopher Columbus. (Speaking of which, it's said that Columbus grew cucumbers in Haiti for pickling purposes.)

Fast-forward to the eighteenth century, and George Washington was known to have a collection of close to 500 varieties of pickles. Shortly after that, industrial-scale pickling began growing rapidly. In the early 1800s, Frenchman Nicolas Appert invented the modern method of canning pickles and other goods by way of airtight containers. He placed food—fruits, vegetables, jellies, syrups, soups, and dairy products—in glass bottles before removing the air, sealing them, and then boiling the bottles. It's why historians call him the father of food science. James Young and John Mason (of the Mason jar) then perfected Appert's invention in the 1850s, and the process hasn't changed much since.

Once pickles were easy to package, interest in the novelty started to spread. At Chicago's World's Fair in 1893, Henry J. Heinz handed out pickle pendants to each fairgoer who stopped by his booth. It's said that he ended up giving away a million pickle pendants.

During the Great Depression of the 1930s, pickles cemented their status as a staple food because of how cheap they were to produce and how long they could be stored. Many struggling Americans stuffed bread and butter pickles between two slices of buttered bread as a low-cost, readily available meal. A peanut butter and pickle sandwich became another go-to dish—and it's a sweet and salty combo that many folks still enjoy today.

Today, pickles are mostly enjoyed for their flavors, with viral recipes popping up all the time. The pickle is so beloved now that it's even beginning to receive star treatment: In early 2025, *Top Chef Masters* contestants were challenged to create gourmet dishes that focused on pickle flavors. What they came up with included everything from grilled octopus with spicy pickle chimichurri to a braised short rib with pickle au jus to a mustard seed tart featuring bread and butter pickles and dill ice cream.

With growing interest and more people brining their own at home, the pickle craze is real.

Refrigerator Dill Pickles

Makes 48 spears

No canning required! These easy pickles are ready to go after just 2 days in the refrigerator. Want spicy dill pickles? Add a couple of sliced serrano peppers to the brine.

- 2 cups white vinegar
- 1½ cups water
- 1 tablespoon coriander seeds
- 1 tablespoon whole black peppercorns
- 2 tablespoons pickling salt
- 1 teaspoon fennel seeds
- 1 bunch fresh dill, roughly chopped
- 12 pickling cucumbers (Kirbys are a good choice here), cut lengthwise into quarters

1. Add all ingredients except dill and cucumber spears to a large nonreactive bowl. Stir and let sit at room temperature for 2–3 hours.
2. Divide dill evenly among 2 or 3 pint-sized glass jars. Divide cucumber spears evenly among jars.
3. Pour pickling liquid over cucumber spears. Screw lids on, and store jars in refrigerator for 2 days before using. Store in refrigerator for 2–4 weeks.

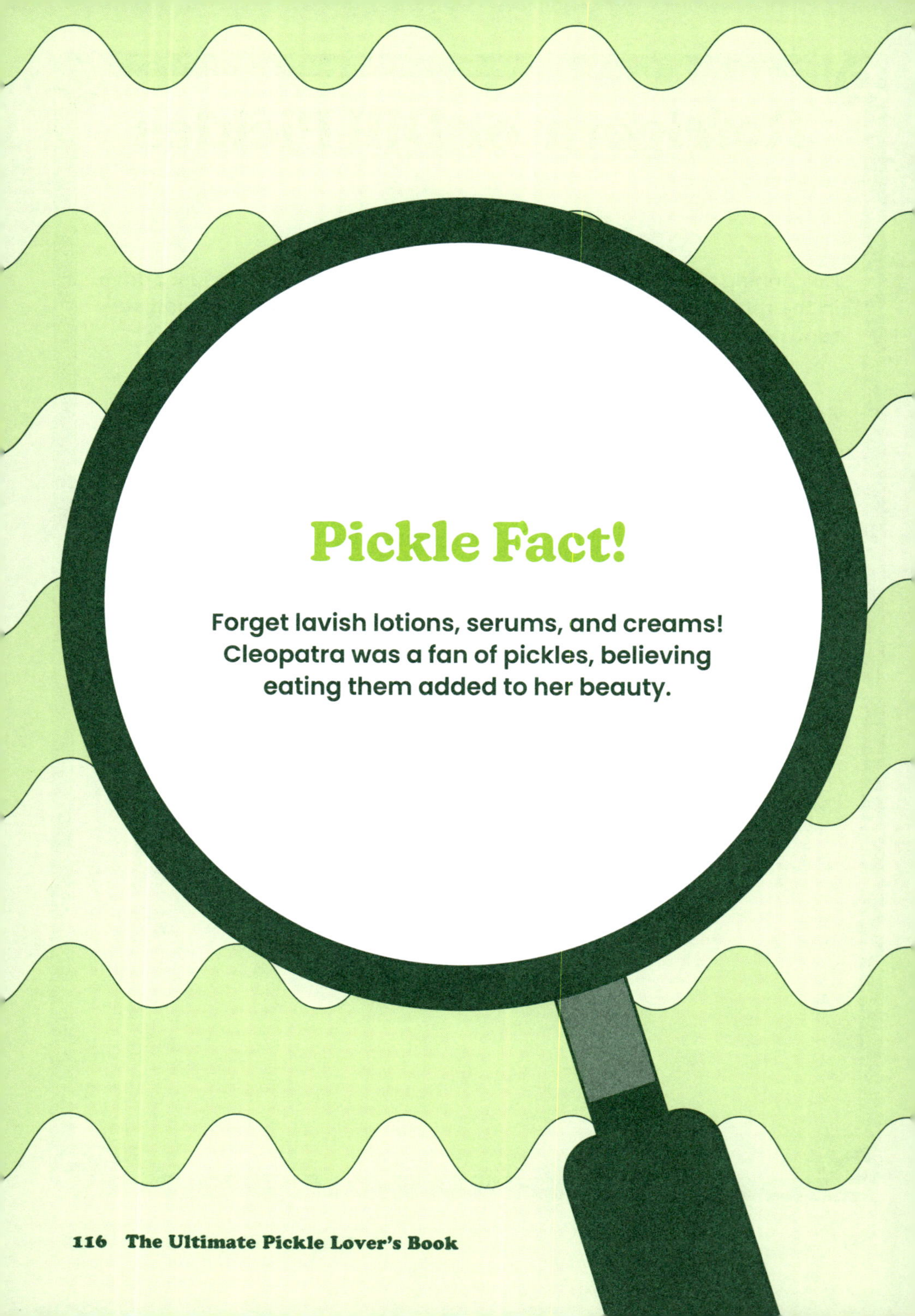

Pickle Fact!

Forget lavish lotions, serums, and creams! Cleopatra was a fan of pickles, believing eating them added to her beauty.

Bread and Butter Refrigerator Pickles

Serves 8

These delicious pickles sport a sweet and sour flavor with just a little kick.

1 pound pickling cucumbers, sliced 1/4" thick
1 small sweet onion, peeled and thinly sliced
1 tablespoon kosher salt
1/2 cup granulated sugar
1/2 cup distilled vinegar
1/2 cup apple cider vinegar
1 tablespoon mustard seeds
1 tablespoon coriander seeds
1 tablespoon whole black peppercorns
3 allspice berries
1/4 teaspoon celery seeds
1/4 teaspoon ground turmeric
1/4 teaspoon crushed red pepper
1/8 teaspoon ground cloves

1. Toss the cucumbers, onion, and salt together in a large nonreactive bowl. Cover with lots of ice and let sit at room temperature for about 2 hours. Discard ice and rinse sliced vegetables in cold water. Drain and rinse a second time.
2. Combine sugar, vinegars, mustard seeds, coriander seeds, peppercorns, allspice, celery seeds, turmeric, red pepper, and cloves in a large nonreactive pot over high heat. When liquid comes to a boil, reduce heat to medium-low and simmer for 5 minutes, then add the cucumbers and onion.
3. As soon as the pot starts to bubble again, remove from heat. With a slotted spoon, transfer vegetables to a 1-quart canning jar. Pour liquid over vegetables. Seal tightly and allow to cool.
4. Once jars are cool, refrigerate for up to 3 months. Pickles are ready to eat once cool, but the flavor will continue to develop for several days.

BRAND SPOTLIGHT

Does Dietz & Watson pride itself on "making handcrafted meats and cheeses The Right Way since forever"? Yes! But don't forget the food company's pickle assortment—every mouthwatering deli sandwich calls for a crunchy pickle or two on the side.

In 1939, young German sausage maker Gottlieb Dietz, who spent years perfecting his original German bratwurst recipe after fleeing post–World War I Germany, purchased The Watson Meat Company from Walter Watson, who stayed on as sales manager. In 1942, Dietz's two teenaged daughters, Ruth and Lore, started working with him. It was Ruth, also known as Momma Dietz, who eventually took the reins, dedicating her weekends and summers to the business. She introduced the company's iconic diamond logo in 1957 and served as chairwoman until she was 94 years old.

Compared to the hundreds of premium meat and cheese varieties that Dietz & Watson offers, its pickle selection has a modest array of fewer than a dozen options. The family-owned company's classic dill seems to be a go-to, thanks to its crunch factor and hint of garlic flavor, but Dietz & Watson also offers half sours and sweet horseradish pickle chips, the latter being an alternative for bread and butter loyalists. For many customers, the crunch alone is enough to lure them away from the popular brands they usually buy.

Many people don't even realize that Dietz & Watson sells pickles, but if you do, chances are that you're probably on your hundredth tub by now.

Which prominent military figure offered 12,000 francs ($300,000 today!) to whoever came up with the best way of pickling and preserving foods?

- **A.** Napoleon Bonaparte
- **B.** Louis-Alexandre Berthier
- **C.** André Masséna
- **D.** Joachim Murat

Answer: A. In 1795, Napoleon Bonaparte was willing to pay thousands for a food preservation method that could feed large quantities of troops. Fifteen years later, Nicolas Appert won the prize. He placed food in bottles before removing the air and sealing and boiling the bottles.

Half Sour Refrigerator Pickles

Serves 8

Half sours are the pickles to reach for when you want that fermented taste without all the effort. For these, you'll need pickling salt, which doesn't contain additives. Most table salt contains iodine and/or other ingredients to prevent it from caking, and these extra elements can result in a cloudy or off-color brine.

- 1 pound pickling cucumbers, sliced 1/4" thick
- 1 large carrot, peeled and sliced into coins
- 2 tablespoons pickling salt
- 1 teaspoon coriander seeds
- 1 teaspoon whole black peppercorns
- 1 teaspoon brown mustard seeds
- 1 bay leaf, broken into 3 pieces
- 1/4 teaspoon celery seeds
- 1/4 cup fresh dill sprigs, lightly packed
- 2 cloves garlic, peeled and halved

1. Soak cucumbers in ice water for 1 hour. Drain. Add carrots and set aside.
2. Mix salt and 2 cups water in a medium nonreactive bowl until salt has completely dissolved. Set aside. In a separate, small bowl, combine coriander seeds, peppercorns, mustard seeds, bay leaf pieces, and celery seeds.
3. In a 1-quart canning jar, place about ¼ of the cucumber and carrot slices. Top with ¼ of the dill, a half-clove of garlic, and ¼ of the coriander spice mixture. Repeat this layering until the vegetables are all in the jar or until the jar is packed full.

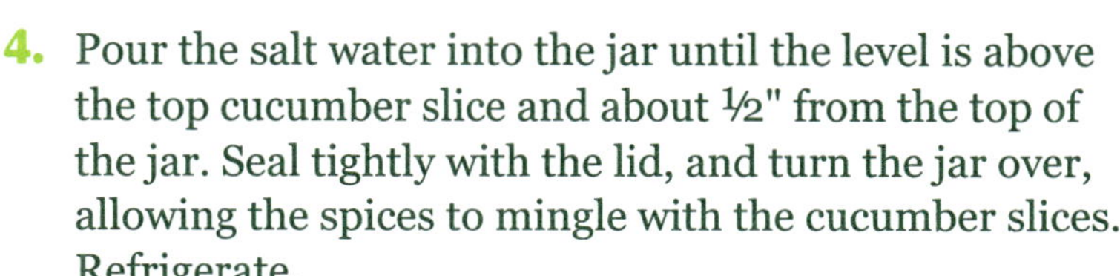

4. Pour the salt water into the jar until the level is above the top cucumber slice and about ½" from the top of the jar. Seal tightly with the lid, and turn the jar over, allowing the spices to mingle with the cucumber slices. Refrigerate.
5. Once a day, turn the jar over a few times to keep mixing the spices with the pickling liquid. The pickles will be ready to eat in as few as 3 days, but the flavor will continue to develop for about a week. These pickles keep in the refrigerator for up to several weeks.

Mustard Pickles

Serves 24

This mustard-infused relish will give you the biggest tangy delight of your life! It's great on hot dogs, burgers, or sandwiches.

- 1 tablespoon pickling or canning salt
- 2 tablespoons granulated sugar
- 2 tablespoons mustard seeds
- 1 cup apple cider vinegar
- 3 cups peeled and chopped cucumbers
- 1 cup thinly sliced white onion

1. Mix salt, sugar, and mustard seeds together in a small bowl; add to a 1-quart jar along with vinegar.
2. Add cucumbers and onions to jar, making sure that all vegetables are covered with liquid.
3. Allow to marinate, refrigerated, for at least 2 weeks before using. Pickles will keep in the refrigerator for up to 1 month.

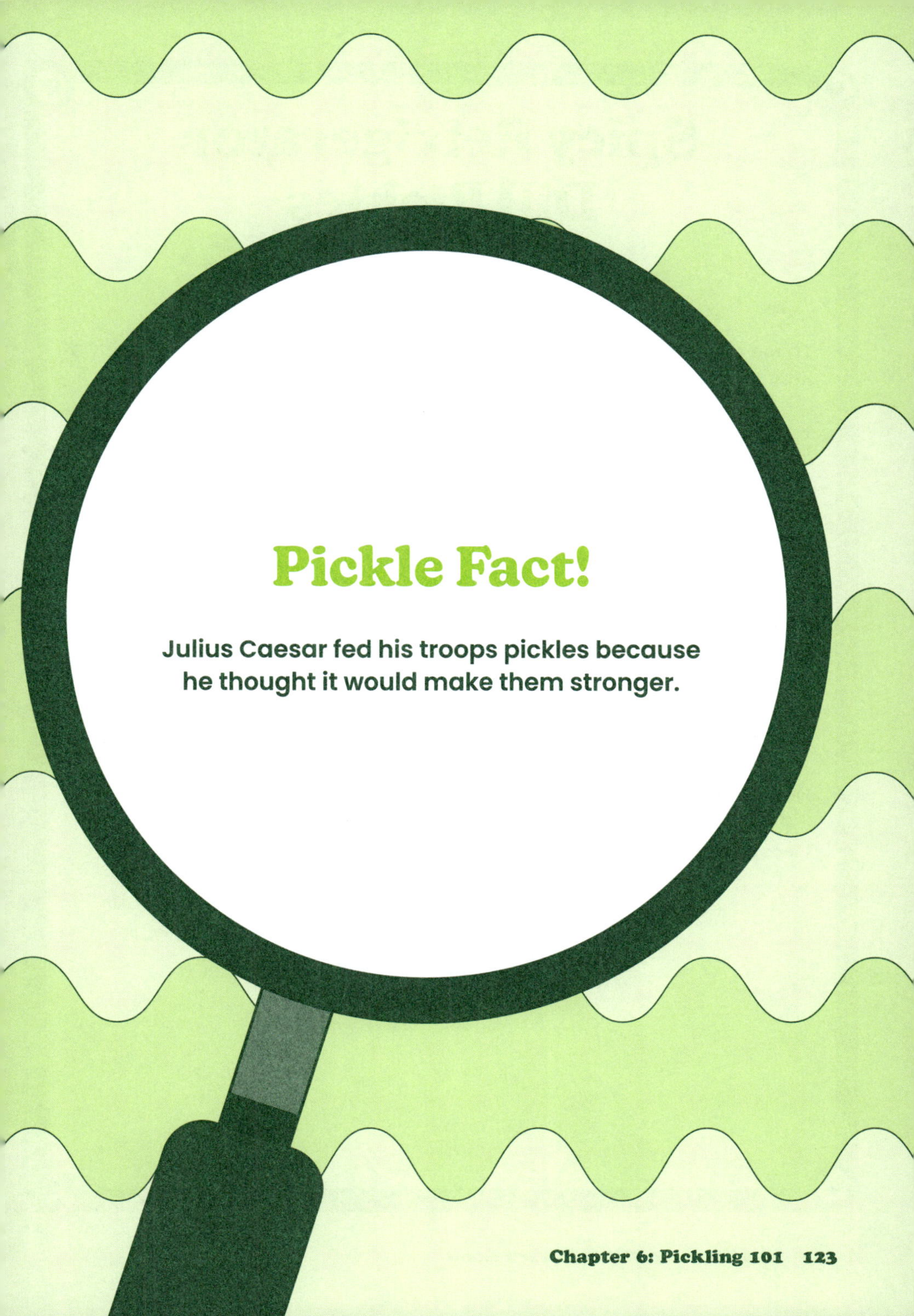

Pickle Fact!

Julius Caesar fed his troops pickles because he thought it would make them stronger.

Spicy Refrigerator Dill Pickles

Makes 1 quart

These crunchy little bites pack a wallop of dill flavor and finish with a little bit of heat.

- **1 pound pickling cucumbers, thinly sliced**
- **6 sprigs fresh dill**
- **1 small red Fresno pepper, sliced**
- **1 cup water**
- **1 cup apple cider vinegar**
- **4 teaspoons kosher salt**
- **1 teaspoon celery seeds**
- **1 teaspoon yellow mustard seeds**
- **1 teaspoon whole black peppercorns**
- **1 teaspoon dill seeds**

1. Pack 2 pint-sized jars with cucumber slices, dill, and pepper slices, leaving at least 1" at the top.
2. Heat water, vinegar, and salt over medium-high heat in a medium nonreactive saucepan. Crush celery seeds, mustard seeds, peppercorns, and dill seeds with a mortar and pestle and add to the brine. Bring brine to a boil. Once salt is completely dissolved, remove from heat.
3. Pour brine into jars to cover vegetables completely. Cover with a clean dish towel or cheesecloth and allow to cool to room temperature. Cover with lids and refrigerate for at least 24 hours. Keeps for 4–6 weeks.

Grow a Pickle Herb Garden

Whether you think you have a green thumb or not, every herb you need to make perfect pickles is right here and can be grown in your own backyard without much effort:

- **Dill.** You can't kick off this list without dill! Cucumber and dill go together like peanut butter and jelly. Bringing an intense, nutty and slightly bitter flavor, dill seeds are ideal for homemade pickles, while tossing in a few sprigs of fresh dill can offset their pungent taste. Although it isn't required, soaking dill seeds the day before planting them is believed to speed up the germination process.
- **Coriander.** The bright, tangy flavor in pickles you enjoy so much? You can thank crushed coriander seeds for that extra zing, so be sure to add this plant to your herb garden.
- **Black, Brown, or Yellow Mustard Seeds.** Beloved for the distinct mildly hot, pungent flavor they bring, mustard seeds are a pickle brine staple for good reason. If spice is your love language, opt for black or brown mustard seeds, but if not, yellow mustard seeds offer a milder profile. It comes down to personal taste.
- **Black Peppercorns.** Don't you feel special when a restaurant server grinds black pepper onto your plate right in front of your eyes? Grinding peppercorns releases piperine, a compound that's responsible for pepper's pungency. As whole peppercorns soak in brine, piperine gets released without overpowering the entire batch of pickles. The longer the peppercorns sit in the brine, the stronger the flavor.

- **Turmeric.** Ever wonder what gives certain pickles their beautiful golden color? A pinch of turmeric powder. Beyond its gorgeous color, turmeric is earthy in flavor while helping to preserve pickles longer. Turmeric is a pretty low-maintenance crop, especially in warm climates. It's usually grown from rhizomes (root-like underground stems) rather than from seeds.
- **Bay Leaves.** Many pickleheads swear that bay leaves are the key to crunchtastic pickles. Natural enzymes in cucumbers cause them to shrivel up and lose their crispness over time. Bay leaves to the rescue! The leaves are high in tannins—compounds that slow those enzymes down and leave you with cucumbers that pack a satisfying crunch for longer.

Winey Briny Pickles

Serves 4

White wine and pickle juice is the pairing you never knew you needed until now! These deliciously boozy pickles make a scrumptious snack. You can also save the brine and add it to cocktails for a savory twist.

- **½ cup champagne vinegar**
- **½ cup white wine**
- **1 teaspoon honey**
- **1 tablespoon kosher salt**
- **½ teaspoon fennel seeds**
- **1 sprig fresh dill**
- **½ pound cucumbers, sliced**

1. In a small nonreactive saucepan over medium-high heat, cook vinegar, wine, honey, salt, and fennel seeds until mixture begins to simmer and salt dissolves.
2. Place dill and cucumbers in a pint-sized jar. Cover with brine. Twist lid on tightly.
3. Refrigerate overnight before using. Keeps in refrigerator for up to 4 weeks.

Pickle Joke!

I watched a documentary last night about how pickles are made. It was jarring.

HA HA

HA HA HA

Freezer Cucumbers

Makes 2 quarts

These pickles can be preserved through canning or through freezing, the latter of which is perfect if you want to enjoy pickles in the winter when fresh cucumbers are harder to come by. Frozen pickles will keep for at least 6–8 months in the freezer. Once you're ready to eat them, thaw them out, and they'll last for about a week.

- 12 cups thinly sliced cucumbers
- 4 cups thinly sliced sweet onion
- 3 cups granulated sugar
- 3 cups white vinegar
- 1 teaspoon pickling or canning salt
- 1 teaspoon mustard seeds
- 1 teaspoon celery seeds

1. Place cucumbers and onions in a large nonreactive bowl.
2. Mix remaining ingredients in a medium nonreactive saucepan; bring to a boil. Stir to dissolve sugar.
3. Pour brine over vegetables. Place a plate on top of vegetables so they remain covered with brine; let sit at room temperature for 24 hours.
4. Move into freezer-safe containers, leaving a small amount of space for expansion in the freezer. Frozen, the pickles will keep for several months.

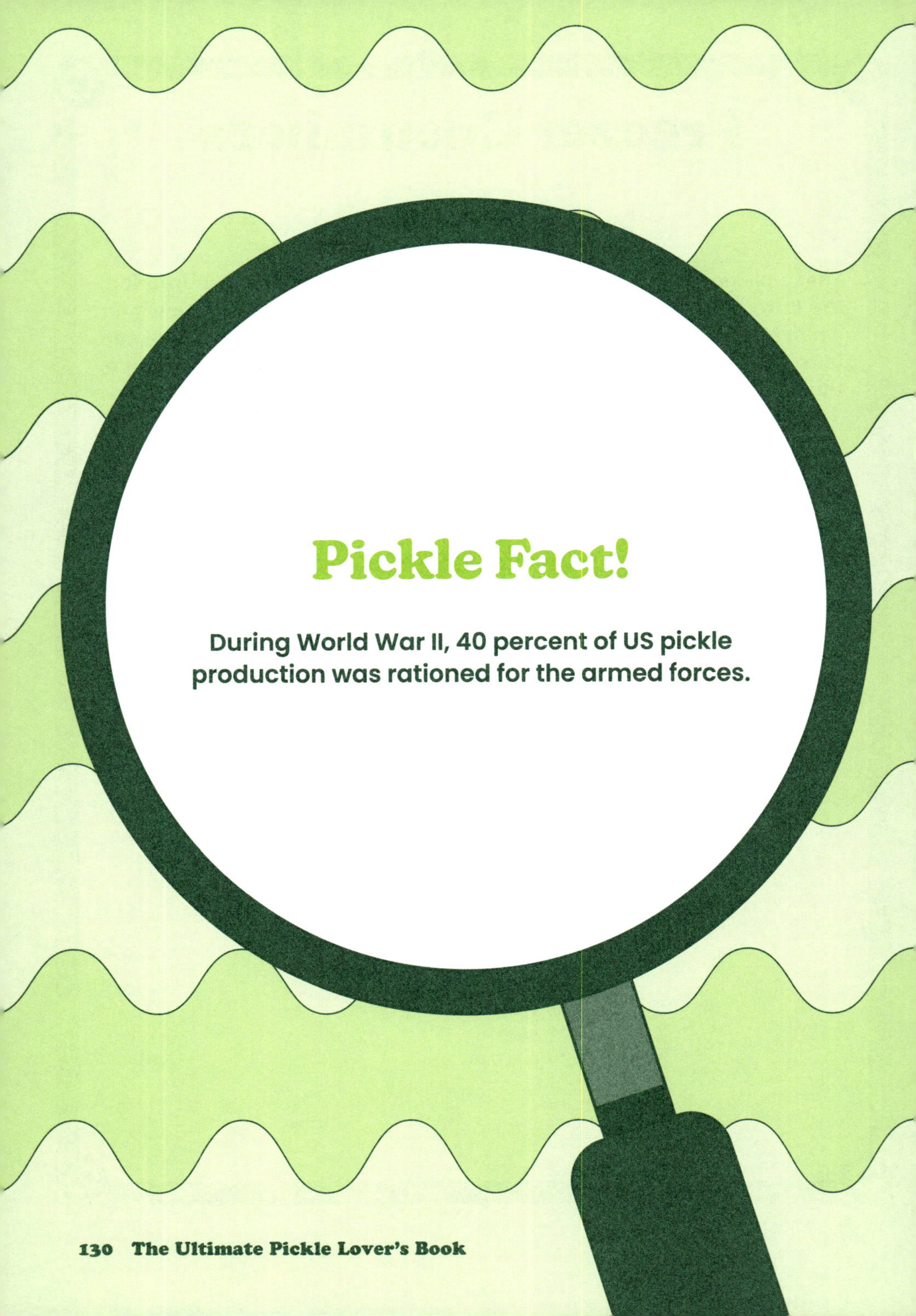

Pickle Fact!

During World War II, 40 percent of US pickle production was rationed for the armed forces.

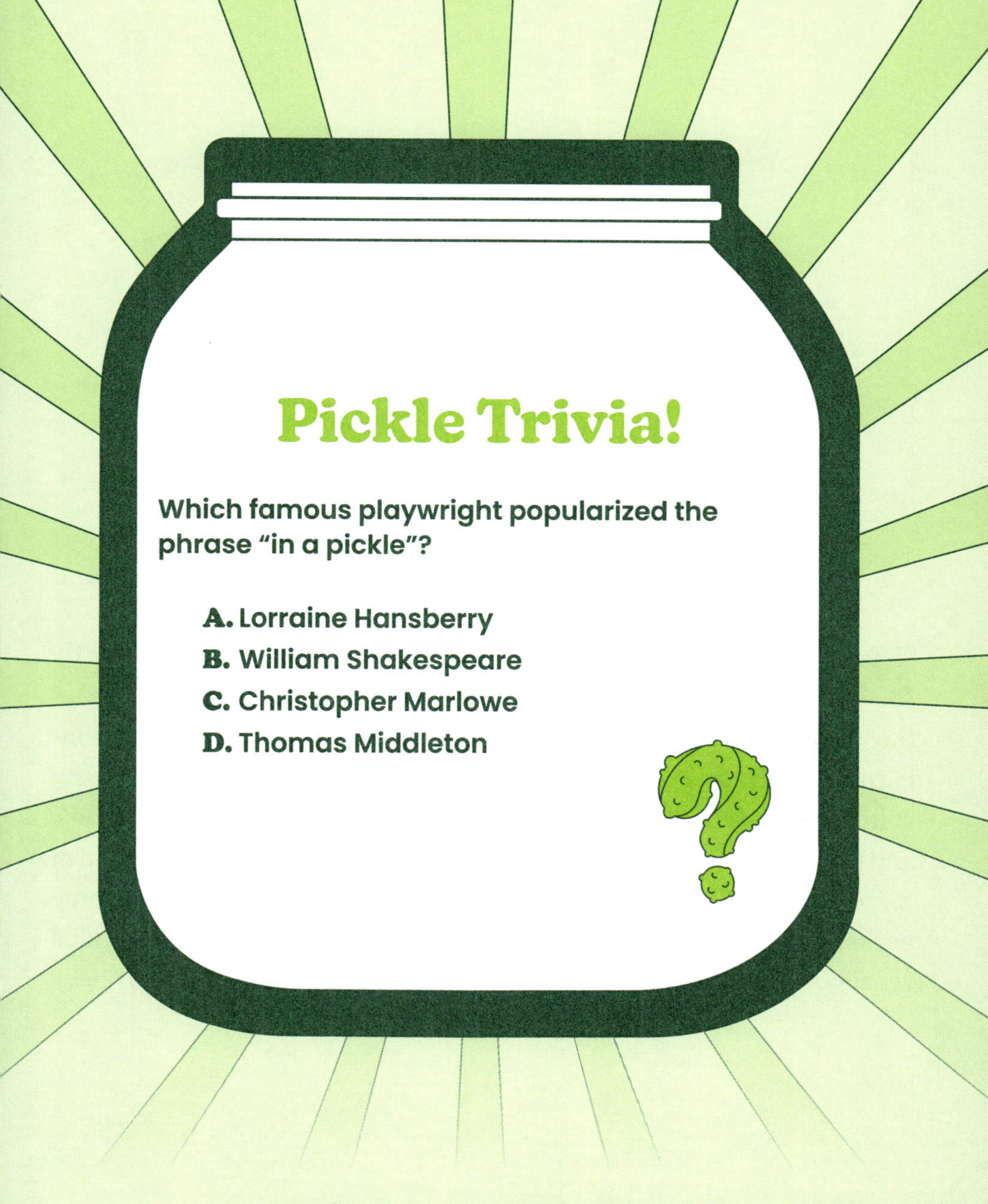

Pickle Trivia!

Which famous playwright popularized the phrase "in a pickle"?

A. Lorraine Hansberry

B. William Shakespeare

C. Christopher Marlowe

D. Thomas Middleton

Answer: B. William Shakespeare coined the phrase "in a pickle" in his 1611 play The Tempest. The line goes, "I have been in such a pickle since I saw you last that, I fear me, will never out of my bones: I shall not fear fly-blowing."

CHAPTER 7

BEYOND THE CUCUMBER

Bryce and Lisa from the hit sketch show *Portlandia* were mostly right when they said anything can be pickled. (Still not sure about those empty CD cases!) This chapter dives deep into the world of non-cucumber pickles, which is full of endless possibilities and exquisite culinary experiences spanning the globe. Dilly beans, preserved lemons, and pickled red onions, jalapeños, and beets? You'll find recipes for all of these and more in the pages ahead. You'll also explore the heartwarming backstory behind Mezzetta, a popular brand for those who enjoy pickled veggies.

Anything Can Be a Pickle!

True pickle lovers know that pickling goes far beyond the cucumber. Apples, blueberries, cranberries, grapes, avocados, plums, watermelon rinds, asparagus, fennel, mushrooms, okra, leafy greens, and even corn on the cob are just some of the fruits and vegetables that can be pickled without a hitch.

Some of the foods you can pickle may surprise you, however. For instance, pickled herring is popular in Sweden, Norway, Denmark, and Finland, as well as eastern Europe. Over in Japan, the tartness of pickled plums (though they're closer to apricots) can perk up a bowl of plain white rice in an instant. And a pickled egg served in a bag of crisps (potato chips) is a pub staple in the UK. (Speaking of classic British cuisine, pairing pickled walnuts with cold meats and cheeses is common at Christmastime.) Pickled sausages served with beer and a slice of dark rye bread are a thing across many Czech Republic bars, while pickled pigs' feet and shrimp are thought of as delicacies in Southern (US) cuisine. Louisiana especially loves Cajun pickled quail eggs. In the Caribbean, pickled pigs' feet (and other parts like the ears and tongue), chicken feet, and even cow trotters are known as traditional "souse."

For those not accustomed to it, pickled meat may be seen as an acquired taste, mostly due to the textural changes that happen during the pickling process—which is why pickled fruits and vegetables are generally more common. When fruits undergo the pickling process, all that yummy, natural sweetness gets enhanced and they become noticeably juicier—especially berries. Pickled fruits pair beautifully with grilled chicken, pork, or duck, as well as ice cream, pound cake, cheesecake, or tarts. Veggies, on the other hand, tend to take on a tangy, delightfully sour flavor that you won't mind puckering up for.

With pickling, you're only limited by your own imagination. Pickled cucumbers are amazing, but you're missing out on a plate chock-full of possibilities and soon-to-be favorites if you think pickling begins and ends with this veggie. As long as you've got the basics—vinegar, salt, sugar, and a few spices—you can turn (almost) anything into a pickled fantasy, so have at it!

Refrigerator Dilly Beans

Makes 1 quart

Tart, crunchy green beans drenched in layers of flavor can take your weeknight salad from drab to fab.

- **2 cloves garlic, peeled**
- **1 pound green beans, trimmed to fit in a 1-pint jar with 1" of space at the top**
- **6 sprigs fresh dill**
- **1 teaspoon crushed red pepper**
- **1 cup water**
- **1 cup white vinegar**
- **4 tablespoons pickling or canning salt**
- **1 teaspoon dill seeds**
- **1 teaspoon yellow mustard seeds**
- **1/2 teaspoon whole black peppercorns**

1. Place 1 garlic clove at the bottom of each of 2 pint-sized canning jars. Pack jars with beans and fresh dill. Top with crushed red pepper.
2. Heat water, vinegar, and salt in a medium nonreactive pan over medium-high heat. Add dill seeds, mustard seeds, and peppercorns. Bring brine to a boil. Once salt is completely dissolved, remove from heat.
3. Pour brine into jars, being sure to cover beans completely. Cover with a clean dish towel or cheesecloth and allow to cool to room temperature. Cover with lids and refrigerate for at least 24 hours. Keeps for 4–6 weeks.

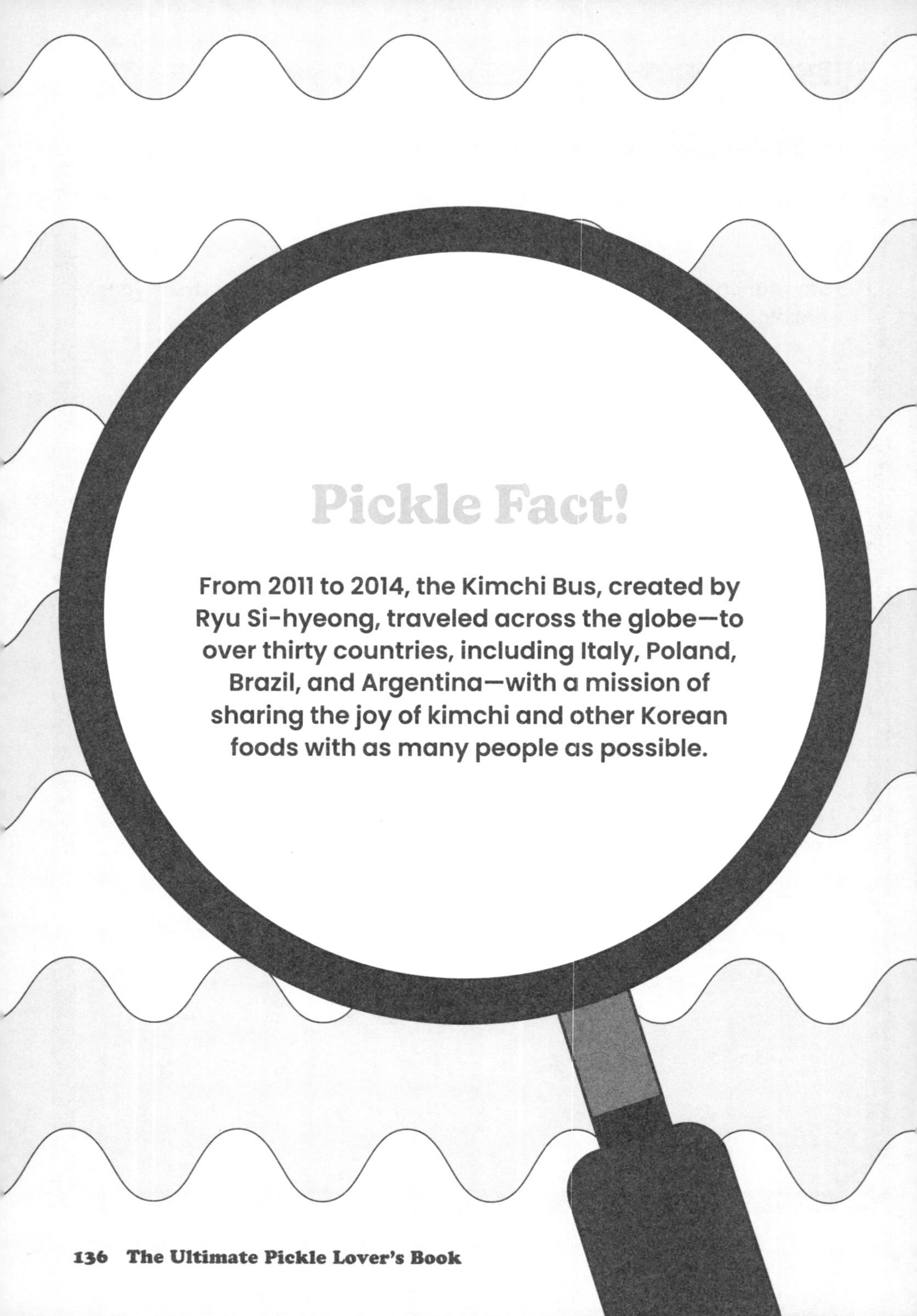

Pickle Fact!

From 2011 to 2014, the Kimchi Bus, created by Ryu Si-hyeong, traveled across the globe—to over thirty countries, including Italy, Poland, Brazil, and Argentina—with a mission of sharing the joy of kimchi and other Korean foods with as many people as possible.

Pickled Red Onions

Serves 8

Crunchy, tangy, vibrantly colored—you can never go wrong with a classic condiment like pickled red onions, whether you're serving up Mexican food, burgers, or grilled steak.

4½ cups water, divided
2 large red onions, peeled and thinly sliced
½ cup white wine vinegar
½ cup honey
1 teaspoon pickling or canning salt
1 teaspoon whole black peppercorns
2 sprigs fresh thyme

1. In a small saucepan or kettle, bring 4 cups water to a boil.
2. Place sliced onions in a large heatproof bowl; cover with boiling water and let sit for 5 minutes; drain.
3. In another medium bowl, whisk together vinegar, remaining ½ cup water, honey, salt, and peppercorns. Add onions and thyme sprigs, and marinate for 10 minutes.
4. Transfer to a jar, cover tightly, and refrigerate until very cold. These pickled onions will keep for several months and get better with age.

BRAND SPOTLIGHT

When you're 5,000 miles away from home, you're bound to feel a little homesick. And when you're homesick, you usually crave all the comfort foods you grew up enjoying, right? That's what happened to Italian immigrant Giuseppe Mezzetta, who moved to the US from Emilia-Romagna, aka Italy's culinary capital. To scratch that comfort-food itch, he took matters into his own hands. In 1935, Mezzetta, who was already working two jobs, and his son, Daniel, started importing specialty olives, peppers, and other Mediterranean staples from Europe and selling them at a North Beach, San Francisco, storefront before wholesaling them to local restaurants.

Fast-forward to present day, and Mezzetta offers everything from unique hot sauces to pasta sauces and marinades that taste like Nonna's homemade cooking. According to their website, Mezzetta's Hot Banana Pepper Rings bring "just the right amount of heat." Meanwhile, the Feta Cheese Stuffed Olives are so yummy that some are tempted to eat the whole jar. But the family-owned brand is probably best known for its giardiniera—a harmonious blend of pickled carrots, celery, cauliflower, and other crisp, colorful veggies. Some can't resist indulging in every last bit of the goodness—down to drinking the juice.

Mezzetta doesn't sell traditional pickles, so if you're looking for dill, sour, or bread and butter pickles, you won't find them—but its jalapeños, peppers, olives, and other California-grown veggies are pickled, brined, and marinated just right. Each product gets harvested and jarred as quickly as possible to ensure that everything is “crunchy crunchy”—because just one “crunchy” isn’t good enough. Mezzetta’s peppers, for instance, are packed within twenty-four hours from the time they’re harvested—more proof of the company slogan, “Mezzetta makes everything betta.”

Pickled Garlic

Makes 2 cups

You're a real one if you can chew pickled garlic without puckering up. If that's you, you'll be happy know that pickled garlic is easy to make on your own and will keep for up to six months in the fridge. Large garlic cloves or whole heads of small spring garlic can be used in this recipe.

6 cups water, divided
1 cup plus 2 tablespoons pickling or canning salt, divided
20 cloves garlic, peeled
1 cup white vinegar
1 cup granulated sugar

1. Combine 4 cups water and 1 cup salt in a large bowl. Add garlic and soak overnight. The salt water should cover the garlic.
2. To make syrup, combine remaining 2 cups water, vinegar, remaining 2 tablespoons salt, and sugar in a medium nonreactive saucepan. Bring to a boil over high heat to dissolve sugar.
3. Let cool. Place garlic in a jar, pour syrup over garlic, and screw on lid. Leave in a warm, dry place (like a sunny windowsill) for 18 days before using. After opening, store in the refrigerator for up to 1 month.

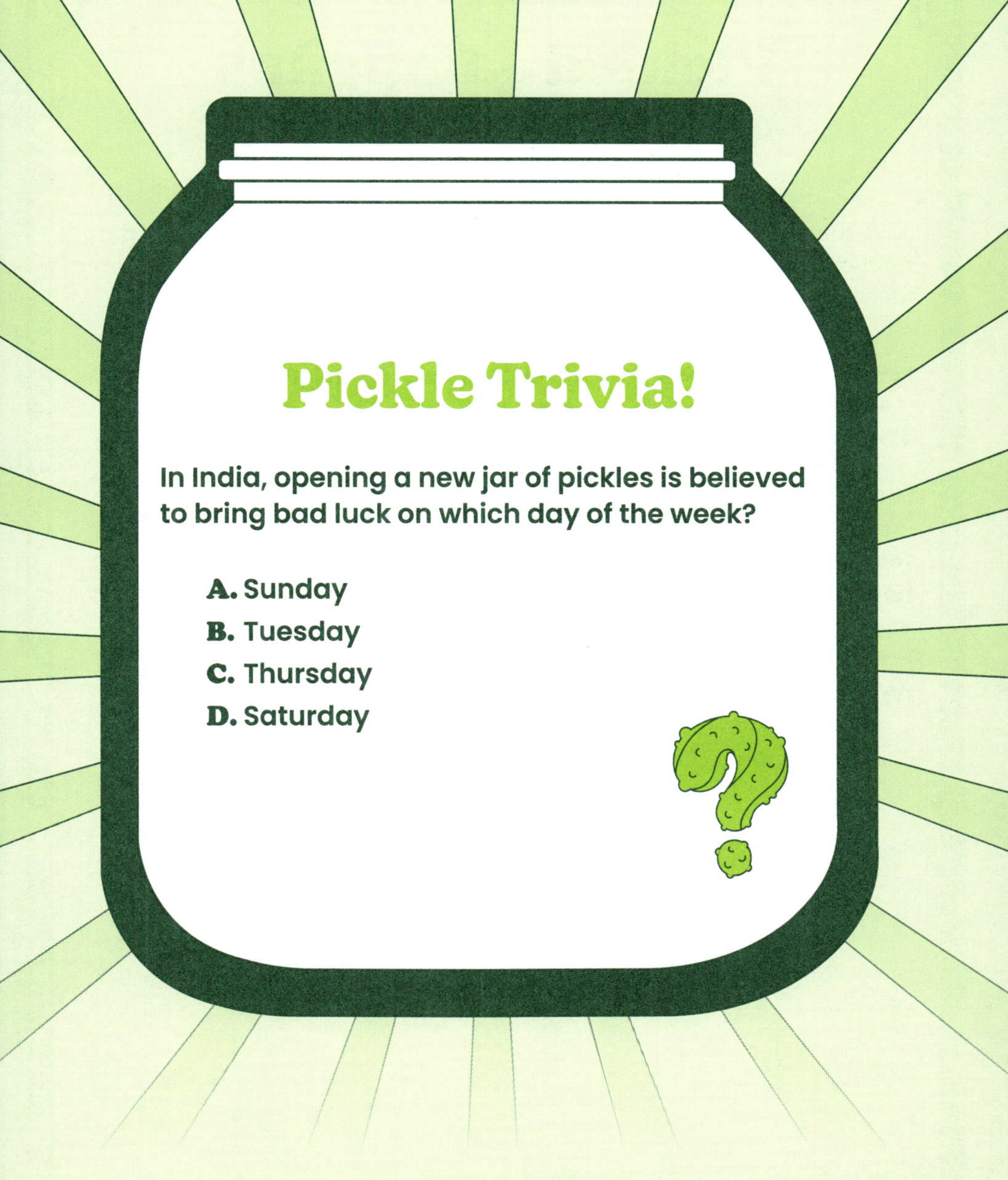

Pickle Trivia!

In India, opening a new jar of pickles is believed to bring bad luck on which day of the week?

A. Sunday
B. Tuesday
C. Thursday
D. Saturday

Answer: B. In India, eating pickles using your fingers, eating pickles at night, passing a pickle jar directly from one person to another, eating the last pickle in the jar, and spilling pickle juice are also believed to bring bad luck.

Pickled Jalapeños

Makes 1 quart

Add these spicy little bites to anything your heart desires. Burgers, nachos, sandwiches, pizza, tacos, and chili are just a handful of yummy ideas.

- **1 pound jalapeños, thinly sliced**
- **2 teaspoons dried oregano**
- **1 tablespoon whole black peppercorns**
- **1 cup water**
- **1 cup white vinegar**
- **4 tablespoons kosher salt**
- **1½ teaspoons granulated sugar**

1. Pack jalapeños tightly into 2 pint-sized canning jars, and top with oregano and peppercorns. Leave at least 1" of space at the top of each jar.
2. Bring water, vinegar, salt, and sugar to a boil in a medium nonreactive pan over medium-high heat. Stir to dissolve salt and sugar. Remove from heat and pour into jars to cover jalapeños.
3. Cover with a clean dish towel or cheesecloth and let cool to room temperature. Cover with lids, and refrigerate for at least 24 hours. Keeps for 4–6 weeks.

Global Pickles

Grab your passport, because there's a whole world of pickled goodies to explore:

- **Kimchi.** A staple in Korean cuisine, kimchi generally consists of napa cabbage and Korean radish that's seasoned with garlic, ginger, and chili pepper powder and then fermented for anywhere between a few days and three years. The result? A sweet, salty, funky, and tangy explosion in your mouth. It's usually served as a side dish with every meal or added to stews. Every year, families get together to make kimchi (a joyous celebration called kimjang) before the winter months to prepare for the cold season ahead and, more importantly, to enjoy the sense of community.
- **Aam ka Achar.** Aam ka achar, also called mango pickle, is a popular Indian condiment made using unripe mangoes, spices, and mustard oil—bringing bold flavor to any dish. It goes great with rice and pairs well with paratha, a type of Indian flatbread, or dosa, an Indian-style crepe.
- **Escabeche.** Looking for a simple way to level up Taco Tuesdays? Look no further than Mexican pickled vegetables. A blend of pickled cauliflower, carrots, jicama, onions, radishes, and jalapeños, escabeche can take your meal from addictive to *highly* addictive. Beyond Mexican cuisine, "escabeche" can refer to a whole constellation of dishes made with vegetables or cooked meats (fish, chicken, pork) marinated in a vinegar-based, spice-infused brine with a hint of sweetness. It's most common across Latin America and the Philippines, but its close relatives also show up in Italy, Greece, Jamaica, and North Africa.

- **Tsukemono.** In Japanese cuisine, a whole rainbow of fresh, pickled veggies are known as *tsukemono* (the literal translation is "pickled things"). Cucumber, daikon radish, eggplant, and ginger are most popular. The veggies are pickled in a brine consisting of salt, soy sauce, miso, sake lees, or rice bran. They're normally served alongside plain rice or miso soup. Every August, a ceremonious event happens at Kayatsu Shrine in Nagoya, Japan, where people pray over vegetables and make tsukemono that's later given to another shrine as a sacred offering.
- **Giardiniera.** The word *giardiniera* means "from the garden." This pickled vegetable mix from Italy resembles a garden, often consisting of roughly chopped bell peppers, celery, carrots, green beans, cauliflower, and gherkins. Brined in vinegar, traditional Italian giardiniera is usually served as an appetizer or snack. Chicago-style giardiniera is preserved in oil after initially being pickled in vinegar, and it's finely chopped, so it's used as a condiment for hot dogs, subs, and pizza. Sport peppers or chili flakes are added to the Chicago-style version for an extra kick.
- **Kabees el Lift.** The quintessential part of any Middle Eastern meal, pink pickled turnips (called *kabees el lift* in Lebanese Arabic) perk up shawarma, kebab, and falafel sandwiches. In fact, a complimentary plate of baton-shaped pink pickles at a Middle Eastern restaurant is a sign of authenticity. Slightly sweet, a tad spicy, and oh, so tangy, pickled turnips add a nice contrast to rich, savory meat dishes. The turnips' bright pink hue comes from beets added during the fermentation process.

Sweet and Sour Beets

Serves 4

These flavorful beets can jazz up any plate with their bright red color. Serve pickled beets with fresh green salad, or as a topping for fancy veggie and grilled cheese sandwiches.

2 medium beets, peeled and cut into 1/4" slices
1/2 cup brown rice vinegar
1/8 teaspoon table salt
1/2 cup apple cider
1 medium bay leaf

1. In a small nonreactive saucepan, cover beets with water. Bring to a boil over high heat. Lower heat and simmer for 15 minutes. Drain. Place beets in a pint-sized canning jar.
2. Bring vinegar, salt, cider, and bay leaf to a boil over high heat, lower heat, and simmer for 2 minutes.
3. Pour vinegar mixture over beets and cover. Refrigerate overnight before using.
4. Drain before serving.

HA HA

Pickle Joke!

Why did the pickled onions wear glasses?

Because they were legally brined!

HA HA HA

Garden Fresh Carrot Pickles

Serves 6

If you have kids, they'll be sneaking these carrot pickles out of the fridge all the time. They're also perfect for serving alongside your favorite Korean dishes.

3/4 cup white vinegar
1 cup water
2 cloves garlic, peeled and chopped
1 teaspoon pickling spice
2 teaspoons kosher salt
2 teaspoons honey
1 pound baby carrots

1. Combine all ingredients in a large nonreactive pot. Cook over medium heat until just boiling.
2. Transfer to a 1-quart canning jar. Place lid on jar. Refrigerate overnight before using, and enjoy within 6 weeks.

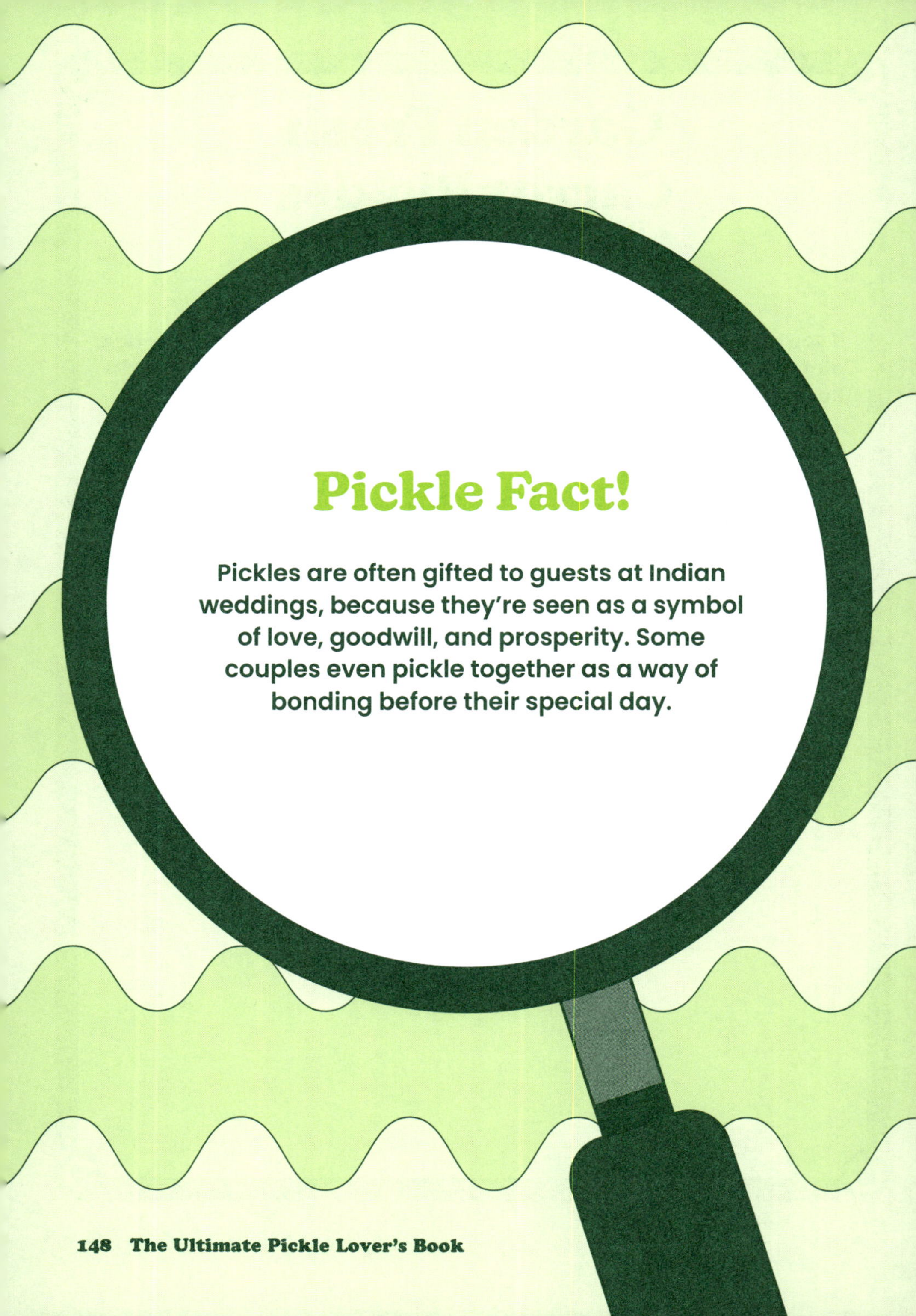

Pickle Fact!

Pickles are often gifted to guests at Indian weddings, because they're seen as a symbol of love, goodwill, and prosperity. Some couples even pickle together as a way of bonding before their special day.

Preserved Lemons

Makes 1 quart

Preserving lemons does magical things to their flavor. They'll wake up just about any dish, from stews to pastas. Just take the lemons' preserved skin and chop it finely. It's especially fantastic in Mediterranean or Middle Eastern dishes.

- **8 large lemons, or 10 Meyer lemons**
- **½ cup pickling or canning salt**
- **4 or 5 sprigs fresh rosemary**
- **½ teaspoon whole black peppercorns (optional)**

1. Cut each lemon open by making two intersecting cuts ¾ of the way through the fruit lengthwise. You should be able to open the lemon up like a flower.
2. Generously coat all surfaces of lemons with pickling salt.
3. Place lemons in a sterilized quart-sized glass jar, compressing them as you go. You're aiming to create a substantial amount of lemon juice in the jar, so don't handle them delicately.
4. Add more salt and lemon juice to cover, if necessary. Add rosemary sprigs and peppercorns, if using.
5. Cap the jar, and allow it to stay at room temperature for 2 days before moving it to the refrigerator. Let the lemons soften for 3 weeks, occasionally shaking the jar to make sure that the juice reaches all of the lemons.
6. To use, remove a lemon, rinse the salt off, discard the flesh inside, and utilize the skin in your recipe. Refrigerate for up to 6 months.

Pickle Trivia!

It's not a Chicago-style hot dog unless there's a pickle! The tradition of placing a dill pickle spear atop the Vienna Beef hot dog is credited to two Jewish immigrants. Where did they hail from?

A. Poland
B. Estonia
C. Germany
D. Austria-Hungary

Answer: D. Originally, the signature Chicago hot dog just had two toppings: mustard and a pickle. Over time, though, as more people came to nineteenth-century Chicago, the veggies started piling on. It's the reason the Chicago-style hot dog is lovingly referred to as being "dragged through the garden."

Perfect Sugar-Pickled Berries

Serves 4

Drizzle these sweet and salty brined berries over angel food cake and top with whipped cream for pure decadence. And the next time you want to impress your dinner guests, serve these gems atop grilled pork or chicken.

- **½ cup champagne vinegar**
- **½ cup champagne**
- **¼ cup granulated sugar**
- **1 tablespoon kosher salt**
- **1 sprig fresh mint**
- **½ pound fresh blackberries and/or blueberries**

1. In a small nonreactive saucepan over medium-high heat, cook vinegar, champagne, sugar, and salt until mixture begins to simmer and sugar dissolves.
2. Place mint sprig and berries in a 1-pint canning jar. Cover with brine. Twist lid on tightly.
3. Refrigerate overnight before using. Store in refrigerator, and enjoy within 4 weeks.

INDEX

D

E

N

O

P

Q

R

S

T

V

W

Y

ABOUT THE AUTHORS

Princess Gabbara is a writer, editor, and pop culture enthusiast with over a decade of journalism and storytelling experience. Throughout Princess's versatile career, her bylines have appeared in and on *Grammy*; *Billboard*; *MTV News*; *Shondaland*; *Bustle*; *Elite Daily*; *Vibe*; *Ebony*; *O, The Oprah Magazine*; and *Essence*. Her career highlights include exclusive interview coverage of celebrities such as Mariah Carey, Jennifer Lopez, Venus and Serena Williams, Dionne Warwick, and Rita Moreno. She is also the author of *I Love Taylor Swift: An Unofficial Fan Journal*.

Kelly Jaggers is a cookbook author, recipe developer, food photographer, food stylist, and founder of the recipe blog *Evil Shenanigans* (EvilShenanigans.com). She is the author of *The Everything® Pie Cookbook*, *Not-So-Humble Pies*, *Moufflet*, *The Everything® Easy Asian Cookbook*, *The Everything® Dutch Oven Cookbook*, *The Everything® Restaurant Copycat Recipes Cookbook*, *The Everything® Easy Instant Pot® Cookbook*, and *Secret Sauce*. She is also a cooking instructor, personal chef, and caterer. Kelly lives in Texas.